THE NAZARITE
Vow

THE NAZARITE

Zachary Hooey

Vow

SOME VOWS ARE
NOT MEANT TO
BE BROKEN

TATE PUBLISHING & *Enterprises*

Published by Tate Publishing & Enterprises, LLC
127 E. Trade Center Terrace | Mustang, Oklahoma 73064 USA
1.888.361.9473 | www.tatepublishing.com

Tate Publishing is committed to excellence in the publishing industry. The company reflects the philosophy established by the founders, based on Psalm 68:11,
"The Lord gave the word and great was the company of those who published it."

Book design copyright © 2008 by Tate Publishing, LLC. All rights reserved.
Cover design by Lynly D. Taylor
Interior design by Stefanie Rooney

Published in the United States of America

ISBN: 978-1-60462-987-3
1. Biblical Study-Life Lessons
2. Vows-Application
08.06.04

Dedication

I dedicate this book to the *Holy Trinity*. *Our Father* [Jehovah], *My Lord and Savior Jesus Christ* [Jehovah], and the *Holy Spirit* [Jehovah]. One God in Three Persons.

I also dedicate this book to my wife, *Irene*, and my two daughters, *Destinee and Lynnsha*–thank you for allowing me to share myself to the world.

I dedicate this book to my grandmother, *Lillian Gains* (1912-1996), my mother, *Gloria Johnson*, my father, *Bobby Joe*, and my aunts, *Nancy* and *Carolyn*.

I want to give a special thanks to the *Calvary Baptist Church*, Salt Lake City, Utah, *Reverend France A. Davis*, Pastor (My father in the ministry).

I also want to give a special thanks to the *Sun City Christian Fellowship Baptist Church*, EL Paso, Texas, *Reverend Earl B. Payton*, Pastor (My second father in the ministry).

Last, but not least, I dedicate this book to Pastor *Chuck Smith* (my grandfather in the ministry), a mighty man of God whom I have not yet had the pleasure of meeting.

May God continue to bless you and the Calvary family of anointed ministers of the gospel of Jesus Christ on the Calvary Satellite Network (CSN radio network).

Without all of you encouraging me...
where on earth would I be?

Acknowledgments

HOOEY HALL OF FAME
Mighty Men of God in My Life

Hanging out in Glory

Dr. J. Vernon McGee (www.ttb.org)

Dr. Adrian Rodgers (www.lwf.org)

Dr. D. James Kennedy (www.coralridge.org)

Alive and Kicking

Pastor France A. Davis (www.calvaryslc.com)

Pastor Earl B. Payton (www.suncitychristian.org)

Pastor Chuck Smith (www.twft.org)

Bishop T.D. Jakes (www.thepottershouse.org)

Pastor John MacAuthor (www.gty.org)

Pastor Chuck Swindoll (www.insight.org)

Dr. Charles Stanley (www.intouch.org)

To Every Man an Answer (www.csnradio.com)

Dr. David Jeremiah   (www.turningpointonline.org)

Pastor Rick Warren   (www.saddleback.com)

Dr. Woodrow Kroll   (www.backtothebible.com)

Dr. R. C. Sproul   (www.ligonier.org)

Moody Bible Affiliates   (www.moodyministries.net)

Justin Alfred – Greek & Hebrew Scholar
(www.wordinlife.com)

Chaplain, Major (Ret) Dale Forrester   (US Army)

Arnie McClatchey   (www.kelpradio.com)

Pastor Eddie Sinegal, Sr.   (www.northeastbfc.org)

TABLE OF *Contents*

Foreword

Behold... I set before you an open door. I am He who opens and no one shuts, and shuts and no one opens. Walk through the open door while you still have breath for I am with you. My rod and My staff shall comfort you. I shall prepare a table before you in the presence of your enemies. Only be thou strong and very courageous. I know the plans I have for you. My plans are to prosper you and to give you an expected outcome. You do not believe you are capable of what I have called you to do, which is okay, this is why I have chosen you.

You are not capable in your own strength, but with My strength, you shall do very well. I own all the cattle on a thousand hills... and I own the hills. Promotion comes neither from the east, nor from the West, nor from the South, but from the North... the place where I dwell. I counsel you to buy of me gold tried in the fire that you may be rich, and white raiment that you may be clothed with My righteousness and not be ashamed when you stand before me. Right now you see through a dark glass, but soon you shall see clearly my plans for you.

Your eyes have not seen, nor have your ears heard, nor has it even entered into your mind all the things I have prepared for you. I just need you to step out in faith. I need you to be strong. I need you to be very courageous. Do not fear him who kills the body only, and after that have no more power [Satan], but fear Me who has the power to destroy both your body and your soul in Hell. The fool hath said in his heart—there is no God. I said to the fool—this day is your soul is required... he believes now... though it is too late for him. Why do the heathen rage and the people imagine vain things? My adversary has blinded them. Be wise therefore, serve Me with fear and rejoice with trembling.

I have made a decree, it is gone out of My mouth and shall not return unto Me void; touch not My anointed servants and do My prophets no harm. Vengeance *is* Mine alone. I will repay all evil done against you. I will make your enemies your footstool. I will never leave you nor forsake you. I will bless those that bless you and curse those that curse you. I give you the authority to tread on the head of serpents and scorpions. All the forces of evil shall fear you, they tremble at My name. All you need is the faith of a mustard seed and you can do all things through Me.

Greater is I who am with you and in you than My adversary who goes around like a roaring lion seeking whom he may destroy. One of My servants said he would not give unto Me that which cost him nothing. I blessed him in his coming in and his going out and I shall do the same for you. Only be thou strong and very courageous.

Behold... I come quickly and My reward is with Me.

Jehovah

Introduction

Dear Friend,

It is my prayer that you will take advantage of the time you have left on this earth. It is my prayer that you will endeavor to bear much *fruit* for the Kingdom of God. Fruit is the result of ministry. Ministry is showing God how much you love Him and are truly thankful for Him sending His Only Begotten Son [Jesus] to die on the cross for your sins. This little book will challenge you to do more for God. It will open up opportunities to serve God in ways you may not have imagined. It is my continuous prayer that you will realize that you are better than blessed, in fact…you are *blessed to be a blessing*. This book is designed to help believers of Jesus Christ to get out of our comfort zone. We tend to become complacent and never achieve a high level of intimacy and unshakable faith in our creator… Jesus Christ. We pass up many opportunities to glorify God by living a selfish life of just dotting the *I* and crossing the *T*. We are selfish by nature and have had to learn how to share with others from our childhood. The Christian life is about sharing; sharing of our time, gifts and talents. It is the afterlife that this book is primarily concerned with. We are all going to die one day and stand before Jesus and give an account as to how we lived our lives since being saved. This little book will help you lay up *treasures in heaven* called rewards! Rewards await every believer in Jesus Christ. All rewards are a result of participation or non-participation in Kingdom building. Some of our rewards shall be burnt up because we did not have the right motives. The only motive is 'love.' The Bible says that while we were yet *sinners* God so loved the world, He sent His only begotten son, Jesus Christ, to die on the cross for our sins. Witnessing is the result of a true relationship with God *without* the promise of a reward. However, God has chosen to reward us for service to Him and it is my prayer that you may bear much fruit for the Master.

Will you travel with me on our way home to heaven and put some treasures on *layaway* until God calls us home?

At the conclusion of your short journey, you will have a deeper *Satisfaction* within your spirit that might not have been obtained without the Vow. You will have entered into *Spiritual Warfare* on behalf of the souls of others. You will have obtained a higher level of spiritual *Discipline*. You will have grown in *Spiritual Maturity*. You will be better able to see the lost through the eyes of God. You will have a better understanding of the *Heart* of God. You will be better able to hear the *Voice* of God. You will have partaked in the *Great Commission* of kingdom building—*and*—not only did you step out on faith, but you also increased your faith. In the final conclusion of life, 'It is only what we do for God that lasts and matters most.'

Reverend Zachary F. Hooey
EL Paso, Texas
August 2007

Chapter I

HEAVENLY
LAYAWAY ACCOUNT

"Lay not up for yourselves treasures upon earth, where moth and rust doth corrupt, and where thieves break through and steal: 20 But lay up for yourselves treasures in heaven, where neither moth nor rust doth corrupt, and where thieves do not break through nor steal: 21 For where your treasure is, there will your heart be also"

(Matt 6:19-21 KJV).

Do you have a *Heavenly Layaway?* A heavenly layaway is an open *'deeds'* account in heaven that gets larger and larger as we mature in Christ and bear fruit for the Kingdom of God. Physically speaking, we go to retail stores, put items on layaway at Wal-Mart and other department stores, and then reduce the amount of the layaway month by month until we pay it off. Spiritually speaking, we put *good deeds* on layaway and we continue to put them on layaway—day by day, week by week, month by month, and year by year until God calls us home. Our physical contributions to our account cease when we die, however, as the gospel seeds we planted in the lives of people and/or the organization(s) we may have started continue to minister to the needs of the community, God still credits you with what fruits resulted from your ministry. For instance, Dr. J. Vernon McGee[1] passed away in the 80's, but his weekly radio broadcast (www.ttb.org) continues on the radio to this day, reaching people around the world and changing lives. I listen to him daily here in El Paso, TX, on the Christian radio station, KELPradio.com. The Apostle Paul's desire for the Christians living in Philippi was that fruit (good deeds) would be added to their heavenly layaway account as they attended to his needs while he was in prison for the gospel of Jesus Christ:

> "For even in Thessalonica ye sent once and again unto my necessity. 17 Not because I desire a gift: but I desire fruit that may abound to your account. 18 But I have all, and abound: I am full, having received of Epaphroditus the things which were sent from you, an odour of a sweet smell, a sacrifice acceptable, well pleasing to God"
>
> (Phil 4:16-18 KJV).

Not only do our heavenly layaway account get larger and larger as we mature in Christ, but the account is never closed until the church is taken out of the world.

This is the doctrine of the Rapture of the Church. The Rapture is an event on God's prophetic calendar that can take place at any moment. In other words, there is nothing that needs to precede it that has been prophesied in the Bible. Everyday, a member of the church, the Body of Christ dies and goes on to be with the Lord. At the Rapture, the whole church body of Christ, still alive on earth, will be taken out. This is what the books and movie 'Left Behind'[2] is all about. At this point, all works cease, then shall the rewards in heaven be given or taken (1 Cor 3:11-15).

> "Behold, I shew you a mystery; We shall not all sleep, but we shall all be changed, 52 In a moment, in the twinkling of an eye, at the last trump: for the trumpet shall sound, and the dead shall be raised incorruptible, and we shall be changed"
>
> (1 Cor 15:51-52 KJV).

In life, everybody is motivated for some type of reward; whether it's a baby screaming at the top of its voice for somebody's attention – or the drug addict who comes up to your car at the stop light and washes your window without even asking and expecting a donation. Our heavenly account is opened when we accept Jesus Christ as our Lord and Savior. The Book of Malachi speaks of our *deeds* being recorded:

> "Then they that feared the LORD spake often one to another: and the LORD hearkened, and heard it, and a book of remembrance was written before him for them that feared the LORD, and that thought upon his name"
>
> (Mal 3:16 KJV).

Everything we do in life is recorded in heaven and written in God's books. Just as credit bureaus have all of your credit history immediately available for any creditor to see, so does God record all of our good deeds in

His *Book of Remembrance*. If you get a chance, check out the movie, *Bruce Almighty*,[3] starring Jim Carey. In that movie, a file drawer on Bruce's life is opened and stretches from one end of the room to the other.

The Book of Revelation talks about books (written on both sides) being opened at judgment day – *and* – the Lamb's Book of Life, out of which those who rejected Christ shall be judged:

> "And I saw a great white throne, and him that sat on it, from whose face the earth and the heaven fled away; and there was found no place for them. 12 And I saw the dead, small and great, stand before God; and the books were opened: and another book was opened, which is the book of life: and the dead were judged out of those things which were written in the books, according to their works. 13 And the sea gave up the dead which were in it; and death and hell delivered up the dead which were in them: and they were judged every man according to their works. 14 And death and hell were cast into the lake of fire. This is the second death. 15 And whosoever was not found written in the book of life was cast into the lake of fire"
>
> (Rev 20:11-15 KJV).

As we can see, there is an account for the saved as well as the unsaved. The heavenly account for the *born again* believer may not start to earn interest and yield dividends for years after he/she accepts Christ... *if at all!* The reason for this is their attachment to the things of this world. Until a believer comes to a saving faith in Jesus Christ and establish an intimate relationship with Him, only then can they produce fruit for the kingdom. A saving faith in Jesus Christ produces *fruit*. This *fruit* is the good deeds of the believer that is consistent with living and witnessing the faith. There are only two types of people in the world today as far as God is concerned... *saved* and *unsaved*. Of the two types, they are broken down in four categories. Christ identifies these four categories in the *parable of the sower*:

"Then He spoke many things to them in parables, saying: "Behold, a sower went out to sow. 4 And as he sowed, some seed fell by the wayside; and the birds came and devoured them. 5 Some fell on stony places, where they did not have much earth; and they immediately sprang up because they had no depth of earth. 6 But when the sun was up they were scorched, and because they had no root they withered away. 7 And some fell among thorns, and the thorns sprang up and choked them. 8 But others fell on good ground and yielded a crop: some a hundredfold, some sixty, some thirty. 9 He who has ears to hear, let him hear!" 18 "Therefore hear the parable of the sower: 19 When anyone hears the word of the kingdom, and does not understand it, then the wicked one comes and snatches away what was sown in his heart. This is he who received seed by the wayside. 20 But he who received the seed on stony places, this is he who hears the word and immediately receives it with joy; 21 yet he has no root in himself, but endures only for a while. For when tribulation or persecution arises because of the word, immediately he stumbles. 22 Now he who received seed among the thorns is he who hears the word, and the cares of this world and the deceitfulness of riches choke the word, and he becomes

> unfruitful. 23 But he who received seed on the good ground is he who hears the word and understands it, who indeed bears fruit and produces: some a hundredfold, some sixty, some thirty"
>
> (Matt 13:3-9; 18-23 NKJV).

The good thing about this parable is that Christ explains it Himself. There is in theology what is called *expositional constancy*. Expositional constancy is when you see a word used in a parable and that word has the same meaning in all parables. In this parable, the Fowls are satanic demonic spirits, the Field is the earth, the Sower is Jesus Christ, and the Seed is the Word of God. We, as people of faith, continue the work Christ began by sowing the same seeds throughout the world.

In this first category, Satan immediately come along and snatches the word out of their hearts. If we think back to when we were a child, we readily received the teachings of our parents no matter what the subject. We believed what our Sunday School teachers taught us and anything the Pastor said. It's not until we get older and learn the ways of the world do our hearts become hard and it is easy to reject the teachings of the Bible as absolute truth. As we witness, Satan is right there to snatch that which was spoken before they even have a chance to process what they heard. This in itself is a testimony to the power of the gospel. Satan will do whatever it takes to keep people from hearing about Jesus' offer of salvation and accepting that offer. This is where you and I come in and step out in faith in evangelism knowing that people are bound by demonic forces. When people reject your offer of salvation, do not take it personally. Satan has every intention of keeping what he has. Truth be known, he did not want to lose you and I to Jesus Christ.

The second category of people in this parable will receive your witness with joy, but they do not have enough faith to stand against a determined foe [Satan] who is determined to have them back. They never developed a solid foundation in their faith. They spend little to no time studying their Bible on their own, attending church and Bible Study, and praying to God daily.

The third category is the one most believers fall into. I will go on record and say about eighty percent of professing Christians fall into this category. The thorns represent the cares of this world that our Father already knows that we have need of. These are the things that please the flesh that many believers find so difficult to separate from–drinking, cussing, sleeping around, getting high off various kinds of drugs, etc. This person has not learned to trust God. They have little to no relationship with God outside of a Sunday church service. They take one step forward and two steps backward.

The fourth person in the parable is the genuine believer in Jesus Christ. We have learned to trust and depend on God. We become doers and not just hearers of the words of Christ. Our *layaway account* is earning interest and yielding dividends. We strive to no longer consciously serve *two masters [sprit and flesh]*. We have come to *love* the one [Christ] and *despise* the other [Mammon]. Mammon is *stuff*. Stuff is anything we put before God. The things we put before God include our spouse, significant others, children, pets, cars, jobs, houses, automobiles, personal effects, self, and wealth (as in the case of the Rich Young Ruler). Many believers do not realize that the love of the world's vain riches is enmity (hatred) against God; and those who do know, can't seem to break the stronghold Satan has on them. In a way, it's kind of an oxymoron when we pray to God and worship the *stuff* we have accumulated. In other words, in spiritual warfare terms, it is an oxymoron when we pray to God in the spirit and worship Satan in our flesh. We do not *physically* bow down and worship Satan, nor call out his name in worship, but our actions dictate who our loyalty is toward.

WORKS

As Christians, we are saved by grace alone. There is absolutely nothing we can do to add to what God has already done by simply believing that Jesus Christ is the only way to the Father—and being dogmatic about it. However, God has decided to reward us for spreading the gospel of Jesus Christ, therefore we work for a reward (1 Corinthians 3:11-15). Many of you may not be receiving this type of teaching on heavenly rewards in your local church, but that's okay because you are receiving it right now. Evangelism is primarily how we receive these rewards. Evangelism is fast becoming a lost art in America. It is vaguely mentioned in pre-printed Sunday School lessons. Vacation Bible School material centers on evangelism, but as a whole, evangelism is scarcely exercised by the church where members go out weekly and knock on doors to spread the gospel. I believe that Pastor's of churches who do not systematically teach the *entire* Bible, from Genesis to Revelation, will be held accountable. When God calls us home, every believer's work shall be made manifest and judged as to what sort it is. This book centers on 1 Cor 3:11-15.

Jesus Christ has commissioned all believers to share the *'good news'* that their sins are forgiven and that they can personally go before the Throne of Grace to obtain favor and get to know God intimately. My definition of favor is… having messed up credit and still getting a car loan or home loan. That's favor!

> "Let us therefore come boldly unto the throne of grace, that we may obtain mercy, and find grace to help in time of need"
>
> (Heb 4:16 KJV).

On God's timetable, we are living in the *Age of Grace*. Christ is our mediator between God and man during this period. The Throne of Grace is the prophetic time in which we live. We will be in this era until the *Times of the Gentiles* is fulfilled (Luke 21:24). I believe this time period will be fulfilled at the Second Advent (the second coming of Christ). Meanwhile, we do not need an intercessor as the Israelites did in the times of the Old Testament prophets and priests who stood between man and God. We can come boldly before the Throne of Grace and petition God for our own needs and heart's desires. Jesus' work of redemption on the cross secured for us a lost fellowship with a Holy God. Not only is our fellowship restored, but we have been commissioned to do good works worthy of salvation. John the Baptist stated clearly to the priests of his day:

> "Then said he to the multitude that came forth to be baptized of him, O generation of vipers, who

hath warned you to flee from the wrath to come? 8 Bring forth therefore fruits worthy of repentance, and begin not to say within yourselves, We have Abraham to our father: for I say unto you, That God is able of these stones to raise up children unto Abraham. 9 And now also the axe is laid unto the root of the trees: every tree therefore which bringeth not forth good fruit is hewn down, and cast into the fire."

(Luke 3:7-9 kjv)

This is not a contradiction to salvation by grace, but an opportunity to express your joy over death and eternal fellowship with God. As we migrate from *Me*ology to *Christ*ology, we express our gratitude by lining our will up with God's will. So then…Our heavenly rewards are the result of the *good deeds* we do when sharing and living our faith as Jesus taught in the New Testament.

"Take heed that you do not do your charitable deeds before men, to be seen by them. Otherwise you have no reward from your Father in heaven. 2 Therefore, when you do a charitable deed, do not sound a trumpet before you as the hypocrites do in the synagogues and in the streets, that they may have glory from men. Assuredly, I say to you, they have their reward. 3 But when you do a charitable deed, do not let your left hand know what your right hand is doing, 4 that your charitable deed may be in secret; and your Father who sees in secret will Himself reward you openly"

(Matt 6:1-4 nkjv).

Our works must be purely motivated… not to be

seen of men, lest we have received our reward in full (a pat on the back, or an *at-a-boy*, or an *at-a-girl*). Works of the flesh (fleshly motivated) is as filthy rags before God. Works led by the spirit of God is what lasts. For this reason, the Nazarite Vow was a private matter between man and God. We must do everything in the power of the Holy Spirit. The work the Father is doing in the world today is not by His power, nor by His might, but by His Spirit. The Holy Spirit gives the spiritual gifts we are to operate within. Jesus Christ is the administrator of the gift(s), and the Father empowers the gift, thus we have the power of the Holy Trinity working in us and through us in ministry (1 Cor 12:4-6). This goal of this book is to motivate you and help you discover what your spiritual gifts are and what God's purpose is for your life. The Jews in the New Testament thought the Pharisees were very *holy* people. They thought that they were very close to God. Jesus sheds light on their relationship with God and calls them hypocrites. The Greek word for hypocrite is *actor*. Actors pretend to be someone or something else. They are role players. In our eyes, they are really good at what they do. In God's eyes, they are as fake as a three-dollar bill. They were no more close to God than any other Jew. In fact, many Jews were healed of crippling and fatal diseases by Christ, whereas the Pharisees received nothing from Christ but a stern condemnation. Their legalism created a burden on the people. Jesus instructs us to come unto *Him* and learn of *Him* and take *His* yoke upon us for His yoke is easy and His burden is light (Matt 11:29-30 KJV).

SWEET SPOT

When we operate within the *sweet spot* of our spiritual gifts, the blessings of God flows through us and we are not frustrated with ministry. The gifts and talents God gives us are not burdensome, but an enjoyment. I have heard pastors who have been pastoring for over twenty years express how they do not feel tired in the least bit, but would like to continue pastoring for many more years. Take heed when asked by the pastor to work on a particular project that you are not equipped for lest you be frustrated in performing it. If it is a burden and frustrates you, and the people around you, you are not operating in your *sweet spot* (ministry gift). Ask the pastor to allow you to step down so that project will not cause you more harm than good. When we operate in our sweet spot, we are refreshed daily. We do not grow weary in well doing. In fact, we enjoy what we do. I believe I have been called to the prison ministry. I have been ministering in prisons since 1999. I started at the Utah State Prison, preaching and teaching Bible Study to men in the Chapel and in Maximum Security twice a week. I have been teaching Bible Study at the Rogelio Sanchez State Jail and Transfer Facility here, in EL Paso, TX, since 2003. I enjoy what I do and I do not feel tired in the least bit nor do I get frustrated. In fact, I prioritize my life around the prison ministry. Everyone has a *sweet spot* in them for ministry. It is not until we fall in love with Jesus and commit to Him, make time for Bible Study and Sunday School, and prioritize our life around kingdom building, do we find our *sweet spot* in ministry. Just worshipping and serving God becomes a *sweet spot* for all believers when we fall in love with God. When we operate in the *sweet spot* of ministry, serving good feels sooooo good; serving God feels natural; serving God becomes second nature. The Apostle Paul operated in his *sweet spot*... as an Apostle to the Gentiles. During his ministry, he was beaten, shipwrecked, snake bitten, stoned by his fellow countrymen, imprisoned–yet, he kept on keeping on. He stated that he had learned to be content in whatever situation he found himself (Phil 4:11). When Paul wrote this epistle to the Philippians, he was chained to a Roman guard, twenty-four hours, seven days a week. He was sustained and comforted by the power of the Holy Spirit and Jesus Christ. The Holy Spirit gives us *staying* power. He helps us run the race to the finish line. He helps us worship the Father in *spirit* and in *truth*. He helps us serve the SON with gladness. He comforts us, He refreshes us, He prays for us, He gives us courage and boldness. Without reliance on the Holy Spirit, our works become *dead* works and are burnt up at the believers judgment. Jesus closes out the Book of Revelation with the promise of rewards for our works:

> "And, behold, I come quickly; and my reward is with me, to give every man according as his work shall be."
>
> (Rev 22:12 KJV)

Chapter 2

THE NAZARITE VOW

THE NAZARITE VOW IS A 'PRIVATE' MATTER

The Nazarite Vow was a private matter between the person making the vow and God. It was a symbol of a life dedicated to God and totally separated from sin. The kind of life Christian believers will live in heaven with God as Jesus presents to Himself a bride without spot or wrinkle (Matt 25:1-13; Eph 5:27; Rev 19:5-9). In the Old Testament, God separated one tribe out of the twelve tribes of Israel, to be His Priests. That tribe was the tribe of Levi, the third son born to Jacob by Leah. They served Him day and night in the tabernacle and later in the temple. The Levites tore down, transported, set up the tabernacle, and performed all of the sacrifices God required of His people. The Levites were full-time ministers to God on behalf of the people. They represented God to the people and represented the people before God. God knew that once His children had gotten to know Him personally and intimately that they would want to serve Him. The Nazarite Vow was a means for those not born a Levite to consecrate themselves for service to Him. If a Jew (male or female) felt that God was calling them into the ministry full-time or they just wanted to consecrate themselves for a period of thirty days or however long they chose, the Nazarite Vow was the means by which they were able to accomplish this. The person who under took the Nazarite Vow did not have access to some of the privileges the Levites were granted while serving in the tabernacle, but it would still be a way of declaring to the people that you were set apart unto God for ministry. You were now going to represent God before the people.

THE FIRST VOW MENTIONED IN THE BIBLE BETWEEN MAN AND GOD

The first mention of a vow in the Holy Bible is between Jacob and God in which Jacob initiated the vow (Gen 28:20). Many people are confused and believe that Jacob tried to strike a deal with God because he was called a *trickster* as his action implied. In the Old Testament, names were given as relating to the circumstances of their birth. Jacob's name means 'heel-catcher' implying that he was trying to keep his brother Esau from being born first. Jacob got the title of trickster because first, he cheated his twin brother Esau out of his birthright, then he tricked his father into giving him his older brother Esau's blessing at his mother's request. The blessing of the first-born in the customs of the Israelites was of great importance. The birthright assured the first-born received two-thirds of what any other son(s) received. The blessing by the father did not necessarily have to go to the firstborn, especially if the firstborn proved himself unworthy of carrying on the family responsibilities. Reuben was Jacob's firstborn son, but he slept with his father's concubine. A concubine is the equivalent of a girlfriend, not a wife. Jacob's vow to God was that, since God promised that He would be with him and bless him, Jacob would in turn give a tenth of his possessions to God as a way of showing his gratitude. You have to do a Hebrew word study to correctly understand what Jacob meant. On the outside looking in, it seems like Jacob wheeled and dealed with God. Later, Jacob would wrestle with an angel, the preincarnate Christ, and would have his name changed to Israel. He wrestled with the angel and he would not give up because he was a strong iron-willed man. Jacob's weakness was his strength. He was prone to rely upon himself rather than to trust in the Lord completely.

In a night when Jacob really needed rest, God sent His angel to wrestle with him all night long. Satan comes at us when we are fatigued and stressed out and plants his thoughts in our minds and we believe we are hearing from God when it is only the king of tricksters himself. This is one reason why we are told to *try the spirit by the spirit* to see if what we are perceiving to be from God is really of God or of Satan (1 John 4:1). Jacob would not give up, he would not surrender his will and gave the angel no choice but to touch the hollow of his thigh and deliberately cripple Jacob. Sometimes I wonder if we deliberately cripple ourselves by insisting that our will be done. Many men are in prison so that God could get their attention before someone or something could kill them and they miss out on an opportunity for eternal life. Thank God he answers the prayers of our mothers and fathers to save us by any means necessary due to our blindness by the god of this world [Satan]. God does not force Christ on us, he gets us to a place where we can make a conscious decision to either accept Christ or reject him. We have this same authority to wrestle men, women, and children from bondage to sin by taking them before God in prayer and allowing God to get them to a place where they can make a conscious decision to either accept or reject Jesus Christ as their LORD and Savior (Luke 10:19). Jacob's one thought was always that he could flee from his brother Esau, but God took that option away from him by crippling him. If Esau had smitten the company of people Jacob sent before him, Jacob could have run and escaped. This is what finally brought Jacob to the place of complete trust in God.

In God's desire to do great things for us and through us, sometimes he has to get us in a position of total dependence on Him. Jacob finally surrendered. That is what God wanted him to do all along, surrender his life, surrender his will unto the Lord. You see, it goes much deeper than what it seems on the outside. God had made a promise to Abraham which was passed onto Isaac and then to Jacob and his children. It *was* and *is* Satan's job to try and make sure God's plan does not come to pass in our life. So then, this was more than just a wrestling match, it was divine destiny for Jacob and salvation for you and I. It is through the Jews Jesus Christ came. It is through the Jews we have our Holy Bible. It is through the Jews we know how God intended for mankind to live amongst each other and in fellowship with Him, and it is through the Jews we have salvation through Jesus Christ. Sometimes a person's greatest strength can be their greatest weakness. God does not want us to depend upon our natural abilities; He wants us to depend totally upon Him. Satan wants us to depend upon our natural abilities. Jacob is a good illustration of what God has to do with some of His children (not all) so that He can do all the things He's been wanting to do for us since we were in our mother's womb (Psalms 139:13-18). According to Hosea, Jacob began to weep and plead with the angel (Hosea 12:2-6). If it wasn't for Hosea, we would think that Jacob was in a commanding position and prevailing over the angel 'not so' Hosea says that he was weeping, he was crying, he was pleading – *please don't go without blessing me* (emphasis mine). The angel asked him what was his name, reminding him of his character; my name is Jacob—heel catcher—because I caught my brother's heel and I've been at everybody's heel. I've been a clever, self-governed man, and a master of my destiny. Therefore, the angel blessed him by changing his name—a change of name meant a change of character. No longer was Jacob a clever heel-catcher, but a man whose life is governed by God. Israel means one who is governed by God. This is the blessing God bestowed upon Jacob. It may not seem like much of a blessing, but it was a complete character change. Jacob was no longer a trickster, as his character implied, but a man whose life was governed by God. He no longer relied on his cunning, but now relies totally on God. This is the place where God wants to get each and every one of His children. The Holy Spirit will do this for us when we're born again (if we let him). We're told in scripture to be transformed by the renewing of our mind (Romans 12:2). Eventually, we will get sick and tired of being sick and tired and allow God to have His way. Let's be thankful that God wrestles with us.

HISTORICAL VOWS

Marriage Vows.[4] Marriage vows are promises a couple makes to each other during a wedding ceremony. In Western culture, these promises have traditionally included the notions of affection ("love, comfort, keep"), faithfulness ("forsaking all others"), unconditionally ("for richer or for poorer", "in sickness and in health"), and permanence ("as long as we both shall live", "until death do us part"). Most wedding vows are taken from traditional religious ceremonies. Touching love poems or lyrics from a love song can be revised as wedding vows. Some couples choose to write their own vows, rather than relying on standard ones spoken by the priest. Marriage vows are not meant to be broken. Regardless of the lack of commitment we see in the world today, God hates divorce:

> "Didn't the LORD make you one with your wife? In body and spirit you are his. And what does he want? Godly children from your union. So guard your heart; remain loyal to the wife of your youth.16 "For I hate divorce!" says the LORD, the God of Israel. "To divorce your wife is to overwhelm her with cruelty," says the LORD of Heaven's Armies. "So guard your heart; do not be unfaithful to your wife."
>
> (Mal 2:15-16 NLT)[5]

Vow of Celibacy. Celibacy refers either to being unmarried or to sexual abstinence. Celibacy is sometimes used as a synonym for "abstinence" or "chastity." A vow of celibacy is a promise not to enter into marriage or engage in sexual intercourse. The term involuntary celibacy has recently appeared to describe a chronic, unwilling state of celibacy. Clerical celibacy is a requirement for priests of some religions or denominations within a religion. These are church laws maintained by the Roman Catholic Church and also by the monastic orders of Hindu and Buddhist traditions. For Christianity, the question of celibacy is handled differently by various Christian authorities. One religious argument for celibacy is given by the Apostle Paul in I Corinthians:

"For I wish that all men were even as I myself. But each one has his own gift from God, one in this manner and another in that. 8 But I say to the unmarried and to the widows: It is good for them if they remain even as I am; 9 but if they cannot exercise self-control, let them marry. For it is better to marry than to burn with passion, But I want you to be without care. He who is unmarried cares for the things of the LORD--how he may please the LORD. 33 But he who is married cares about the things of the world--how he may please his wife. 34 There is a difference between a wife and a virgin. The unmarried woman cares about the things of the LORD, that she may be holy both in body and in spirit. But she who is married cares about the things of the world--how she may please her husband. 35 And this I say for your own profit, not that I may put a leash on you, but for what is proper, and that you may serve the LORD without distraction."

(1 Cor 7:7-9; 32-35 (NKJV)

Catholics understand celibacy to be a reflection of life in Heaven, and a source of detachment from the material world, which aids in one's relationship with God. Catholic priests are called to be espoused to the Church itself, and espoused to God, without overwhelming commitments interfering with the relationship. Catholics understand celibacy as the calling of some, but not of all.

Vow of Chastity. Chastity, in many religious and cultural contexts, is a virtue concerning the state of purity of the mind and body. The term is most often associated with refraining from sexual intimacy, especially outside of marriage. *Chastity* is often taken to be synonymous with virginity or abstention from all sexual activity; however, some consider sexually active married couples to be *chaste* if they have relations only with each other. Due to the prohibitions of sexual intimacy outside of marriage in Abrahamic religions deriving from the Ten Commandments and Mosaic law, the term has become closely associated with premarital sexual abstinence in Western culture. however, in the context of religion, the term remains applicable to persons in all states, single or married, clerical or lay, and has implications beyond sexual temperance. Chastity is one of the Seven holy virtues of Catholic teaching, opposing the deadly sin of lust. The Catechism of the Catholic Church states that "chastity" is the successful integration of sexuality within the person and thus the inner unity of a human person in his or her bodily and spiritual being.

BIBLICAL VOWS

Hannah vowed a vow to God for a child:

"So Hannah rose up after they had eaten in Shiloh, and after they had drunk. Now Eli the priest sat upon a seat by a post of the temple of the LORD. 10 And she was in bitterness of soul, and prayed unto the LORD, and wept sore. 11 And she vowed a vow, and said, O LORD of hosts, if thou wilt indeed look on the affliction of thine handmaid, and remember me, and not forget thine handmaid, but wilt give unto thine handmaid a man child, then I will give him unto the LORD all the days of his life, and there shall no razor come upon his head."

(1 Sam 1:9-11 KJV)

She was barren and grieved to her heart because she could not have children.

Year after year she went to the temple and prayed to God for a child, but it was not until she vowed a vow to God that her prayer was answered. Her prayer was specific... for a man-child (son). Her vow was that she would give him back to God if he opened her womb. I cannot imagine taking my child, my first-born, to the temple and leaving him there – but Hannah kept her vow! After all her years of praying and pleading with God, to finally have her prayer answered, then give him to Eli (the High Priest) after he was weaned. *Wow...* what a blessed woman to keep her vow! She recognized that if it wasn't for God, she would not have had a child at all... so she gave him back to God. Many of us forget God when he answers our prayers. We give His glory to the doctor's or the medicine or some other person whom God may have used to help us stand again on solid ground. We tend go back to life as usual, forgetting God's deliverance—just like the Israelites. This is one reason we go to church week after week: to be constantly reminded of who God is, what He has done in our life and the lives of others, what He is doing, and what He is going to do for His children. Sometimes we may wonder why God wants us to praise Him twenty-four seven, but the truth of the matter is, if our minds are not focused on God then our minds will be focused on the things of this world that gets us out of the will of God.

The Israelites cried unto God for deliverance from slavery. When God led the Israelites out of Egypt, the mixed multitude (Egyptian's who came out with the Israelites after seeing God's mighty works) cried to Moses for leeks and onions, garlic and cucumber's (condiments) and fish that they freely ate when they were in Egypt. What they forgot was the slavery God had delivered them out of. Their backs were bent over from the heavy burdens they were made to carry for over 400 years. Supposedly, many of the great monuments in Egypt were built by the Israelites. They had started to walk deformed (bent over), but they forgot all of that in the wilderness wandering. Egypt represents spiritual bondage—slavery to a hard taskmaster—Satan. Jesus tells of a woman whom Satan had bowed over for eighteen years before Jesus *loosed* her (Luke 13:12). Bishop T. D. Jake's, *Woman Thou Art Loosed, book* and *movie* has set many people free of spiritual bondage to the cares of this world.[6]

Truth be told, the taste of Egypt's *leeks* and *onions*

is still in the mouth of many Christians today. Jesus speaks of His church as becoming lukewarm. Lukewarm is a mixture of hot and cold… just like the mixed multitude. In other words, people who come to Christ still have the taste of the world in them. They have not yet denied themselves, taking up their cross, and are following Jesus. They seek to follow Jesus apart from the cross, apart from *self-denial*. They have just enough Jesus in them to be unsatisfied with the *stuff* the world has to offer and more than enough of the world in them to be satisfied with following Jesus. This type of Christian produces a nominal, surface commitment to Christ:

> "These people draw near to Me with their mouth, And honor Me with their lips, But their heart is far from Me."
>
> *(*Matt 15:8 KJV*)*

Jesus cannot stand *lukewarmness*. He wants our life to be fully crucified with Him. This means a life consecrated for service to the Master. We are not our own, we have een brought with a price on the cross:

> "I know your works, that you are neither cold nor hot. I could wish you were cold or hot. So then, because you are lukewarm, and neither cold nor hot, I will vomit you out of My mouth."
>
> (Rev 3:15-16 KJV)

The mixed multitude's murmuring caused murmuring in the whole camp. Lukewarm believers are not satisfied with only the Word of God, they want to be entertained when they come to church. Some pastors of churches appeal to their flesh to keep them from voting with their feet. Voting with their feet means that if they do not like what the pastor is teaching or his vision for his church, they will leave and find another church. There is always a church out there that will tell them how good they are.

JEPHTHAH' VOW

Jephthah vowed a vow to God for victory. Jephthah's vow was not well thought out which cost him dearly. His vow to God was for victory over Israel's enemies, the Ammonites. In exchange for victory, he would offer to God as a *burnt offering* whatsoever was first to meet him out of his house (small lambs, goats and dogs were pets in many Jewish homes). *Whatsoever* leads me to think that he was thinking of an animal, however, his daughter was the first to come out to greet him! Can you imagine... daddy's little girl!

> "Then the Spirit of the LORD came upon Jephthah, and he passed over Gilead, and Manasseh, and passed over Mizpeh of Gilead, and from Mizpeh of Gilead he passed over unto the children of Ammon. 30 And Jephthah vowed a vow unto the LORD, and said, If thou shalt without fail deliver the children of Ammon into mine hands, 31 Then it shall be, that whatsoever cometh forth of the doors of my house to meet me, when I return in peace from the children of Ammon, shall surely be the LORD's, and I will offer it up for a burnt offering"
>
> (Judges 11:29-31 KJV).

Ohhhh... how special our daughters are to us men.

I share with men that they should see their spouse as *daddy's little girl* (God's daughter) and they better treat her right. Not only was she Jephthah's daughter, but she was his only child! What's Jephthah to do–keep his Vow? Just like Hannah... he kept his vow! Here is the beauty of raising up a child in the way they should go as we see Jephthah's daughter comforting him:

> "And she said unto her father, Let this thing be done for me: let me alone two months, that I may go up and down upon the mountains, and bewail my virginity, I and my fellows. 38 And he said, Go. And he sent her away for two months: and she went with her companions, and bewailed her virginity upon the mountains. 39 And it came to pass at the end of two months, that she returned unto her father, who did with her according to his vow which he had vowed: and she knew no man. And it was a custom in Israel, 40 That the daughters of Israel went yearly to lament the daughter of Jephthah the Gileadite four days in a year"
>
> (Judges 11:37-40 KJV).

Some believe that he actually sacrificed her and burnt her as a burnt offering before the Lord, however, that does not line up with scripture. First of all, only the priest could conduct the burnt offering and that was only done at the temple. Second, God specifically commanded the Israelites not to conduct human sacrifices. Third, it clearly states that she lived a life of consecration to God. In other words, she remained a virgin for life. To know the significance of this, you must know that every Jewish woman wanted to be the woman who brought Jesus into the world. This is why

Hannah wanted a child so bad. Women who were barren were looked down upon in ancient Israel. A Burnt Offering was an offering of consecration in which the whole animal (hide and all) was burnt on the brazen altar to God. This meant a life of total separation to God. Jesus was our burnt offering on the cross. In obedience to her father, she helped her father keep his vow to God.

As Christians, we are to live a life separated unto God for good works, which is our reasonable service. Thus, the Nazarite Vow was one of gratefulness. It was a *voluntary* and *private* matter between the person taking the vow and God.

THE NAZARITE VOW WAS NEITHER A DIET NOR A FAST

Those who took the Nazarite Vow must abstain from certain foods. This mandate was given by God Himself. I will go into detail a little further. Keep reading. For those of you who take a Vow of Commitment, I do recommend a fast during the first week of the month for 1 – 3 days for spiritual strength and renewal. You must be prayed up or you will give up. Do not let the devil cheat you out of your heavenly rewards while you're here on this earth. In other words, do not let Satan rob you of an intimate experience with God of your own undertaking. He will make it his mission to derail you and steal your joy. Follow up the first week of the month fasting with a 12 hour weekly fast once a week. During your fast, pray specifically for the people you are ministering to. Pray specifically for your Pastor's vision and for the leaders in your church to walk in the spirit and not in the flesh. Pray for your church's specific needs. Pray for gang strongholds to be broken, pray for America to repent of her sins of *gross idolatry* and *immorality*. Pray for our Soldiers' salvation, our politicians' salvation, for Israel's salvation, for your family member's salvation, and for Christian morals in your community. Go about your daily duties drawing no attention to yourself while you are performing your vow. Kindly reject certain foods and drinks offered by co-workers, family, and friends. You will need to tell your spouse about your intent to take the Vow of Commitment for support and maybe even your best friend who will encourage you and keep what you are committing to themselves. Ladies, if your husband objects, you cannot take the vow. Remember, it is God who sees what is done in secret and rewards openly. At Sun City, we have an intercessory Prayer Team that meet at the church weekly to pray for these specific needs mentioned above.

Try to coincide your weekly fast to end after the weekly Bible study at your church (after Bible study, *'eats on!'*). After Bible Study, on your way home, have your favorite meal or desert! As you can see, the Vow of Commitment can be rewarding in many ways—and along the way, you will pick up some good habits for life. During your vow, ditch the TV as much as possible. Watch the news and Christian programs. Continuously fill your mind with the things of God. You will be surprised what the Holy Spirit will bring back to your remembrance while you are ministering. Change your radio station to a Christian radio station that offers biblical teachings, or listen to sermons of your pastor or other men and women of God. Constantly fill yourself with the Word of God. Too many Christians only listen to Christian music in their vehicles, at home, and on the job. This works to the devil's advantage. In this way, it takes years before Christians can move from milk, to mash potatoes, to hamburger, to steak & lobster (the meat of the Word of God). Music is great for devotion, but the Bible states that we should *study* to show ourselves approved unto God (2 Tim 2:15) and to be able to give an account of what we believe to any person who asks (1 Peter 3:15). Jesus used the Word of God against Satan during His temptation after His forty days of fasting in the wilderness. If the devil has to compromise, he would surly rather have all Christians constantly listening to Christian music instead of studying the Word of God. One of the ministries of the Holy Spirit is to recall all things back to our remembrance, but we have to put something in our memory for Him to recall it:

> "But the Comforter, which is the Holy Ghost, whom the Father will send in my name, he shall teach you all things, and bring all things to your remembrance"

> (John 14:26 KJV).

Chapter 3

ME-OLOGY VS
CHRIST-OLOGY

"No man can serve two masters: for either he will
hate the one, and love the other; or else he will hold
to the one, and despise the other. Ye cannot serve
God and mammon"

(Matt 6:24 KJV).

*Me*ology is the study of 'Me'. *Christ*ology is the study of
Christ. *Me*ology implies, 'If *I* love *me*, *I* must do what
makes *me* happy.' *Christ*ology states, 'If *you* love *Me*
[Christ], *you* will keep *My* commandments' – and just
what is the commandments of Christ...that we love the
Lord our God with all of our heart, all of our soul, all of
our mind, all of our strength, and to love one another
as He has loved us. *Christ*ology Christians (Christians
walking in His footsteps) are not just hearers, but are
also doers of the word of God.

If we look at the story Jesus tells of the Rich Young
Ruler (we do not have the pleasure of his name, therefore he represents rich people in general) we can see

clearly *me*ology at work in him and the stronghold
money can have on anyone of us who do not acknowledge that all good things comes from above [God]:

> "And a certain ruler asked him, saying, Good Master,
> what shall I do to inherit eternal life? 19 And Jesus
> said unto him, Why callest thou me good? none is
> good, save one, that is, God. 20 Thou knowest the
> commandments, Do not commit adultery, Do not
> kill, Do not steal, Do not bear false witness, Honour
> thy father and thy mother. 21 And he said, All these
> have I kept from my youth up. 22 Now when Jesus
> heard these things, he said unto him, Yet lackest
> thou one thing: sell all that thou hast, and distrib-
> ute unto the poor, and thou shalt have treasure in
> heaven: and come, follow me. 23 And when he heard
> this, he was very sorrowful: for he was very rich.
> 24 And when Jesus saw that he was very sorrowful,
> he said, How hardly shall they that have riches enter
> into the kingdom of God! 25 For it is easier for a
> camel to go through a needle's eye, than for a rich
> man to enter into the kingdom of God. 26 And they
> that heard it said, Who then can be saved? 27 And
> he said, The things which are impossible with men
> are possible with God. 28 Then Peter said, Lo, we
> have left all, and followed thee. 29 And he said unto
> them, Verily I say unto you, There is no man that
> hath left house, or parents, or brethren, or wife, or
> children, for the kingdom of God's sake, 30 Who
> shall not receive manifold more in this present time,
> and in the world to come life everlasting."
>
> (Luke 18:18-30 KJV).

In this story, the rich young ruler represents *'good
people'*. There are many *good people* who think that they

will go to heaven when they die simply because they are good law-abiding citizens; they get along with their neighbors, and they are generous with their substance. They will surely get a chance to plead their case before God on *Judgment Day*. The process is basically the same way we treat those who break the law and get arrested. We apprehend law breakers and throw them in jail where they have to wait to see the judge to be fined, imprisoned, or released. Problem is, at *that* judgment (the Great white Throne Judgment) – no one is saved! I am sure the rich young ruler's parents were very proud of him and I believe he was admired by all the town's people, however, Jesus points out his one problem in life, which was his relationship with God. His relationship with God was not perfect.

Jesus mentions the second section of the Ten Commandments to the rich young ruler which pertained to mankind co-existing with each other; all six of which he kept from his youth (vs20). The first section of the Ten Commandments has to do with mankind co-existing with God. By keeping the commandments concerning man, he surely would have been considered an outstanding member of the community. Problem is… God was not the center of his life. His wealth was the center of his life. The pursuit of wealth and pleasure is the center of many believer's life in Jesus Christ. Here is wisdom. Here is how to get wealth:

> "This book of the law shall not depart out of thy mouth; but thou shalt meditate therein day and night, that thou mayest observe to do according to all that is written therein: for then thou shalt make

thy way prosperous, and then thou shalt have good success."

(Josh 1:, KJV).

This *me*ology way of thinking causes many believers to never enter into the fullness of joy God wants for His children. The grip the world has on us that we don't seem to want to let go of causes many believers to wonder in the wilderness instead of fully entering into the promised land. The Promised Land represents the abundant life in Christ every believer can have at this very moment. Like the Rich Young Ruler, too many people forget we all have a date with death, which could happen at any moment. This appointment with death (the ratio is one per person) is one we all too often put on the back burner until faced with a sudden death experience like a traffic accident or some serious illness we develop either because of our life style or something like cancer that creeps upon us unawares. When confronted with giving up his wealth, the rich young ruler went away sad. How tragic it is to gain the wealth of the world just to lose your soul to eternal separation from God. The biblical definition of death is—separation from God. If God is not the head of our lives and the motive behind all that we do, we have received our reward in full—which happens to be the applause of men. My pastor, Pastor Earl B. Payton, once preached this text and concluded from the 22nd verse, that this rich young ruler could have been the 13th Apostle. Let me ask you a question: which is the greater blessing – having plenty of money and all the nice things this world has to offer, or surrendering all that you have and following Jesus? This is not a difficult question for self-centered people. A more sure question to ponder is, if you died today, would you not have surrendered all that you have to someone anyway?

I like the two extremes between the blessings God gave Abraham's two sons Ishmael and Jacob. To Ishmael, father of the Middle Eastern oil moguls (Saudi Arabia), God gave *Oil*. To Jacob, father of the Jewish nation, God gave the *Bible*. Who got the better blessing... Ishmael or Jacob? Considering the *me*ology world in which we live today and the pursuit of wealth, it appears Ishmael got the better blessing... *or did he?* Through Jacob, we have God's Holy Word, His promises in times of trouble, blessings and curses on the obedient and disobedient, the future of mankind, and salvation through His son Jesus Christ. Isn't it amazing how everything is not what it seems. God has chosen the foolish things of the world to confound the wise.

Many people, if not all, get a sense of urgency after the age of forty. We take seriously the fact that many of our dreams and promises have not been kept. Promises we have made to ourselves, friends, loved ones and maybe even – God! God always seems to be the last on our list of things to do. Women who want a baby and have not had one by age forty start to panic; women who are unmarried and really want to have another baby start to panic not knowing if they will find their *Mr. Right* in time. In my opinion, having lived 45 years, single men start to panic around fifty wondering if they will find their *Mrs. Right* before they get too settled in their ways. It seems as though we get a sense of urgency about so many things after age forty except judgment day and the handing out of rewards (or loss thereof).

Thank God He can still teach an 'old dog' new tricks. What I mean by that is, if we allow God, He will transform our way of thinking to put Him first that He may give us the desires of our hearts. In this *meology* world in which we live, we have put limits on God. Dr. Carroll Baltimore once preached a message, 'Take the limits off God.' In his message, he documents how God has written the laws of reaping and sowing into the tapestry of our faith in giving a potion of our possessions back to God. Deuteronomy confirms that it is God who gives the ability to make wealth:

> "And thou say in thine heart, My power and the might of mine hand hath gotten me this wealth. 18 But thou shalt remember the LORD thy God: for it is he that giveth thee power to get wealth, that he may establish his covenant which he sware unto thy fathers, as it is this day."
>
> (Deut 8:17-18 KJV).

*Me*ology implies I am self-sufficient. I can open doors to my future and I can close them. The casual drinker believes he/she can quit at anytime. The alcoholic knows it is a day-by-day process of denying their flesh to stay off the bottle. The casual drug user thinks they too can quit anytime they want, but the man or woman who has lost everything, including family, knows that only a higher power [God] can keep them when their flesh doesn't want to be kept.

*Me*ology implies I am my own God. A manmade *god* is a powerless little god made in the imagination of man; having hands, but cannot hold, having eyes, but cannot see, having feet, but cannot walk. It has a nose, hands, feet, and eyes—yet, if I made him, he is less than me. I am more intelligent than *he* because I made him. Why then do I serve him (mini-me) and not the real deal? *Me*ology is vanity. Vanity is pride. God hates pride. When we die, our corpse is worth about $1.99, yet we put expensive perfume and expensive clothes on it. Now, there is nothing wrong with putting nice things on our body, in fact, it makes us feel good about ourselves. God wants us to look good and feel good about ourselves—but, like the rich young ruler, these things are not to be the center of our joy. If you lost everything tomorrow, would you still worship God... or would you charge God foolishly with your demise?

God wants to *ridiculously* bless us in this life. In fact, concerning our livelihood, there is only one place in the Bible where God says *Try Me:*

> "Will a man rob God? Yet ye have robbed me. But ye say, Wherein have we robbed thee? In tithes and offerings. 9 Ye are cursed with a curse: for ye have robbed me, even this whole nation. 10 Bring ye all the tithes into the storehouse, that there may be meat in mine house, and prove me now herewith, saith the LORD of hosts, if I will not open you the windows of heaven, and pour you out a blessing, that there shall not be room enough to receive it."
>
> (Mal 3:8-10 KJV, emphasis mine).

If we but seek first the kingdom of God, instead of seeking first our own needs, we'll find that serving the true and living God [Jehovah] yields greater rewards physically, mentally, financially, spiritually, emotionally, and eternally. God will give us the desires of our hearts when we put Him first. The second part of Malachi 3:11, states that God will rebuke the devourer for their sakes. The devourer was the locust that ate everything green upon the land. God wanted to bless His people, but their priorities were wrong. His Priests, the Levites, were supported by the tithes, gifts and offerings of the people. This analogy can be applied to the church today because the preacher is to be paid by the flock he ministers to. The place of worship has its bills to pay and ministries need to be supported to equip the saints. However, the church is not limited to the tenth. Jesus has raised the bar (so to speak) by promising that if we give, it will be given back to us, good measure, pressed down, shaken together, and running over (Luke 6:38). In the Old Testament, it was the Lord of Host [first person of the Trinity] who made the promise of financial and crop blessings. In the New Testament, it is Jesus [second person of the Trinity] who makes the promise of financial blessings (Luke 6:38, 1 Cor 9:6-8). Both Old and New Testament giving was centered on faith. God doesn't need a tenth of anything we have. He already owns everything. That which we have is a gift from God. If we remember back in Deuteronomy, it is God who gives the ability to make wealth that we may have something to give back. The principle of the giving is to support the work of God. Giving is tied to obedience and worship. A cheerful giver testifies to his/her own obedience, subjection to, and reliance on God.

The prophet Haggai prophesied for only two months in Judah. The people had forsaken the rebuild-

ing of the temple in favor of building their own houses
and God was not pleased:

"Then came the word of the LORD by Haggai the
prophet, saying, 4 Is it time for you, O ye, to dwell
in your cieled (paneled) houses, and this house
lie waste? 5 Now therefore thus saith the LORD of
hosts; Consider your ways. 6 Ye have sown much,
and bring in little; ye eat, but ye have not enough;
ye drink, but ye are not filled with drink; ye clothe
you, but there is none warm; and he that earneth
wages earneth wages to put it into a bag with holes.
7 Thus saith the LORD of hosts; Consider your ways.
8 Go up to the mountain, and bring wood, and build
the house; and I will take pleasure in it, and I will
be glorified, saith the LORD. 9 Ye looked for much,
and, lo, it came to little; and when ye brought it
home, I did blow upon it. Why? saith the LORD of
hosts. Because of mine house that is waste, and ye
run every man unto his own house. 10 Therefore the
heaven over you is stayed from dew, and the earth is
stayed from her fruit. 11 And I called for a drought
upon the land, and upon the mountains, and upon
the corn, and upon the new wine, and upon the oil,
and upon that which the ground bringeth forth, and
upon men, and upon cattle, and upon all the labour
of the hands."

(Hag 1:3-11 KJV).

When we neglect spiritual matters, before we get
too far gone, God will send a warning. The devourer
was not rebuked in this instance. The devourer was
God himself and the elements were His rod for punishment. The people never prospered. They simply *got
by*, like many of us do from payday to payday. Though

they ate and drank, they were never satisfied and the kicker is... they never figured out why until God sent His Prophet.

Check out this next verse of scripture!

"And every one that hath forsaken houses, or brethren, or sisters, or father, or mother, or wife, or children, or lands, for my name's sake, shall receive an hundredfold, and shall inherit everlasting life."

(Matt 19:29 KJV).

While searching for *Mr/Mrs. Right*, first establish intimacy with God through prayer and the study of His word—then shall all things be added unto you. The last part of this verse states a hundred-fold blessing *and* eternal life! Guess where the hundred-fold blessing takes place—Yep, that's right—right here on earth! Please do not confuse this *hundred-fold* blessing with the *'name it and claim it'* prosperity teaching where you go and lay you hands on a Cadillac and claim it in the name of Jesus. After you lay your hands on it and claim it in the name of Jesus... then go and run your credit to see if you qualify for it. You may need to go and lay your hands on a Ford Escort. These *hundred-fold* blessings promised by God are tied to 'Ministry.' Ministry is serving Christ. Christ came to seek and to save the *lost*. The lost (unsaved men and women) has not experienced God like you and I who have accepted Christ as our Lord and Savior. I compare the lost to a man who have never had a best friend whom he can tell all his secrets to, his goals, his hurts (etc...) – *or* – a woman who have not experienced the joy of childbirth. The stretching of the body, wondering what it will look like, the joy of finding out if it's a boy or girl, wondering what you're going to name it, wondering what it will be when it grows up, etc. The lost have not experienced what genuine believers in Jesus Christ have experienced. When we practice *Christ*ology, we walk in the footsteps of Christ. We are able to bless hundreds, if not thousands of people in our lifetime with the good news of the Gospel of Jesus Christ. I compare this opportunity to be a huge blessing to hundreds, if not thousands of people to Bill Gates. Bill Gates can bless people financially more than most of us can. What we offer is not material and seems to be the lesser of the two. In the physical realm, who would *not* like to be Bill Gates long lost son or daughter? The reason we would like to be his long lost son or daughter is for the financial inheritance. Well... guess what? As Christians, we get to give the keys to the Kingdom of God to anyone who will receive them by sharing Jesus Christ. Now who has the greater wealth–Bill Gates or You?

Hopefully, you have heard it said that, 'It is only what we do for Christ that lasts.' As New Testament Christians, no longer under the Law (as the Jews still are who have rejected Christ), we have been blessed with 'All Spiritual Blessings' in the heavenlies:

> "Blessed be the God and Father of our LORD Jesus Christ, who hath blessed us with all spiritual blessings in heavenly places in Christ."
>
> (Eph 1:3 KJV).

Where Christ is, we are also. Christ is in heaven and seated at the right hand of God. Christ is also in us by way of the Holy Spirit. So then... not only is

God in us as we walk this earth, but we are with God in heaven. At anytime, privately or publicly, we can go boldly before the throne of grace, either on our knees in prayer, on our jobs, or while driving. We cannot only go before the Throne of Grace on our own behalf, but also on behalf of others. Therefore, you and I are *blessed to be a blessing* unto God, and empowered to minister to the spiritual needs of others. It has always been and always will be what we do for Christ that lasts – it just took a while for God to get us to see that. There is nothing on earth more fulfilling than ministry. Our young skin will wrinkle, our body parts shall sag, our muscles shall droop, our hair shall turn white, our eyes shall grow dim, and our teeth shall fall out... *cheer up*... we shall get a new body, better that this one, when we get to heaven. Fact is, it's the *Christ*ology in us that has a lasting effect on all those we come in contact with. They will tell their children about Christ and their children will tell their children about Christ, and so forth and so on... the same way so many of us have been introduced to Christ through the years.

I grew up in the church, but walked away from God when I joined the Army at the age of seventeen. What I really did was wonder in the wilderness for seventeen years until I re-dedicated my life to Jesus Christ on 26 December 1996, while stationed at Schofield Barracks, HI. One Sunday morning after church, Deacon Samuel McKeown invited me to Sunday School. We were attending the AMR Gospel Service where Chaplain (MAJ) Dale Forrester was the pastor. Chaplain Forrester was white and we were shocked to receive a white preacher. Talking about uphill battles, he was

bald and white and we were a black congregation–yet–
we received him and blossomed under him. He was
like Caleb and Joshua, not afraid of the challenge. In
fact, he had all the deacons teach the Midweek Service. Needless to say, some of the *teaching* deacons later
became *preaching* deacons who later became ministers
(myself included). How dare I not include Chaplain
Forrester, an ordinary unknown man, in my *faith hall of
fame* from which my ministry journey began under his
watch. We were indeed–*blessed to be a blessing*–by this
man of God.

Chapter 4

WHAT DOES GOD REQUIRE

"He hath shewed thee, O man, what is good; and what doth the LORD require of thee, but to do justly, and to love mercy, and to walk humbly with thy God."

(Micah 6:8 KJV).

God's first requirement is that we be saved. The Gospel of Jesus Christ is the *ONLY* means of salvation. A Vow of Commitment is *not* a means of salvation. If you are reading this book and you are not sure if you are saved--STOP--Let's get you saved first! Salvation is putting faith in the atoning work of the Cross which Jesus Christ hung, bled, and died on for *your* sins and after three days, God raised Him up and rewarded Him with *all* power over Heaven and Earth (Matt 28:18-20).

What then is the Gospel of Jesus Christ?

The Gospel of Jesus Christ is believing that Jesus Christ *alone* is the only way to heaven (John 14:6). The Gospel means *Good News* and the good news is that you can be saved *right now*--right where you are--by believing and confessing Jesus Christ as your 'Lord and Savior!'

To do this, we must travel down the Roman road to the Book of Romans:

"But what does it say? "The word is near you; it is in your mouth and in your heart," that is, the word of faith we are proclaiming: That if you confess with your mouth, "Jesus is LORD," and believe in your heart that God raised him from the dead, you will be saved. For it is with your heart that you believe and are justified, and it is with your mouth that you confess and are saved."

(Roman 10:8-10 KJV).

If you are not sure and want to know for sure that you will go to heaven when you die, just repeat after me:

LORD *Jesus, I am a sinner and I want to be saved,*

I believe that You are the only begotten son of God [Jehovah],

I believe that You died on the cross for my sins,

I believe that the Father raised You up on the third day,

Please, come into my heart and save me from my sins.

That's It!

That's the simplicity of the Gospel of Jesus Christ. There are no hoops to jump through as with other religions. By *hoops* I mean that you do not work for your salvation. By grace are we saved through *'Faith'* in Jesus Christ, not of works, lest any man/woman should boast in the presence of God (Eph 2:8-9). In other words, no man has seen God at anytime. The Israelites had seen an appearance of Christ in the Old Testament, but never God the Father. The Father, by faith, wants us to know him even though we cannot see him. For this purpose, He sent His only begotten Son, Jesus Christ into the world to show Him to us. So then, not only can we see the Father, but we can know Him and what He desires for our lives. I was listening to the Christian radio station here in El Paso, TX, KELP, AM 1590, to the Christian program *To Every Man an Answer*.[7] It was during the week of the 9th through the 13th of July 07, and a caller asked the question, 'how do we know if God has healed us when we was sick or if our healing was a natural function of the body or the medicine'? My answer was… faith! I know it is easy to say faith, but that did not fully answer the man's question. In addition to the evidence that our eyes are witness to—and the transformation of our lives and the lives of others, we can clearly see an intelligent creator in the atmosphere, the earth, and the seas. We also have a more sure witness… biblical Prophesy. Prophesy is history written in advance. Only God knows the future and He reveals the future to His servants… Holy Men and Women (the only thing that makes us Holy is the Blood of Jesus). Prophesy proves the physical existence of God even though He is a spirit and we cannot see Him (John 4:24 KJV).

This Christian *faith* journey is to be a bold one even though we have not visibly seen God in person. Jesus said, 'If you are ashamed to confess me in the presence of men, I will be ashamed to confess you before My Father in heaven.' Here is a good explanation of what that means: if someone says to you that they believe there are many ways to God, your response should be... that's not what I believe, my Bible teaches me that Jesus is the way, the truth, and the life and no man *or* woman comes to the Father but through Him. This then would be a statement of your faith in Christ whom you have submitted your life. If you wanted to defend your statement, simply remind the person you're communicating with that out of all the religions in the world, Christianity is the only one whose *prophet* or *good person* (as some religions see their spiritual leader) died on the cross for the sins of the world. Also tell them that Christ is the only who clearly stated all through the scriptures that He is the Son of God. One step further would be to tell them that religion is a one-way ticket to *Hell*, and that Christianity is a relationship with God.

Keep in mind that we are not in the business of forcing people to believe in Jesus Christ. Freely man walked away from God in the Garden of Eden and freely must man walk back to God. Sharing the Gospel is *warfare* with the devil [Satan]. If we go around ticking people off, they will avoid us like the plague. If they avoid us like the plague–who has won the spiritual battle... Satan! As long as he can keep his people in spiritual bondage and away from the truth of the gospel–he has won the spiritual battle for the mind. So then, as we walk this faith journey, we are to be wise as a serpent and as gentle as a dove.

The name Jesus in New Testament times was a common name just as Jesus is a common name here in El Paso, TX. What God has simply done is taken a common name (with a very special meaning: YHWH

[Jehovah] is Salvation) in Jesus' time, and exulted it above every name of human origin, power, principality, dominion, and kingdom; that at the name of Jesus [Christ is a title, not a last name], every knee should bow and every tongue confess, to the glory of God the Father, that Jesus Christ is God.

It is by the Holy Spirit we confess Christ as *God*. As our Great High Priest, Christ makes intercession for us because we are still in this flesh and the accuser of the brethren [Satan] accuses us before our Father in Heaven day and night. For this reason, Jesus taught us to pray to the Father and not directly to Himself, for He intercedes for us and we are to end our prayers in Jesus' name (Matt 6:9-13). Truth be told, the Holy Spirit prays for us because we pray amiss. We pray selfish prayers that are designed to please our flesh:

> "Ye ask, and receive not, because ye ask amiss, that ye may consume it upon your lusts."
>
> (James 4:3 KJV).

> "The Spirit also helpeth our infirmities: for we know not what we should pray for as we ought: but the Spirit itself maketh intercession for us with groanings which cannot be uttered. 27 And he that searcheth the hearts knoweth what is the mind of the Spirit, because he maketh intercession for the saints according to the will of God."
>
> (Romans 8:26-27 KJV).

Chapter 5

THE COMMITMENT

"A Righteous Commitment Is A Calculated Choice."

Earl B. Payton, Pastor

The Nazarite Vow was *your* desire to do something out of the ordinary for God! A Vow of Commitment is similar to the Nazarite Vow except we are not under the Law. A Vow of Commitment has the same desire to serve God in a special way. It is different from a call to preach, teach, or whatever it might be that you believe God's purpose is for your life. It is a desire to consecrate yourself before God for a specific purpose and period of time that *you* decide. I call it *Special Duty*. In the military, we are sometimes given special duty assignments that lasts for a short period of time. One summer in 1984, while stationed in Pusan, Korea, I was assigned to *special duty* at the public swimming pool on main post during the summer (need I say I did not complain). I give this example as a way of saying that something good can and will come out of committing yourself to God for a specific amount of time. The Nazarite vow was a vow for a specific period of time. I recommend no shorter than six months, a year would be ideal. The Nazarite Vow was a vow of personal commitment between you and God in which *you* initiate the vow. Normally, when God calls someone into the ministry, it is God initiating the call and therefore it is God who sustains those whom He calls. In contrast, you are initiating this vow with God, therefore *you* sustain the conditions of the vow for the specified period of time that *you* choose.

It is better not to make a Vow than to make one and not keep it!

I separated the above statement because of its importance. The Book of Deuteronomy clearly states that:

> "If you make a vow to the LORD your God, do not be slow to pay it, for the LORD your God will certainly demand it of you and you will be guilty of sin.
>
> But if you refrain from making a vow, you will not be guilty. Whatever your lips utter you must be sure to do, because you made your vow freely to the LORD your God with your own mouth."
>
> (Deut 23:21-23 KJV).

I want to clearly express that a Vow of Commitment is purely voluntarily and *not* a means of salvation. The reason you might want to make a vow to God in this *'Age of Grace'* is because of *complacency* and *procrastination*. A vow can even be used to prevent you from *not* doing something God has told you to do. In other words, we can *not* do something we feel God is calling us to do by second guessing God. A vow can *jump start* you into action. The devil wants us to second guess God. I have heard so many preachers say that you have to doubt your doubts until faith emerges. A vow is only intended to *jump start* your faith into action. It is so easy to get caught up in the cares of this world that we become ineffective Christians for Christ. We get caught up in 'The Comfort Zone'. While in our comfort zone, we become useless to God and covet with the things of this world. We get so busy with our job and family activities that we may genuinely want to do more for God, but just can't find the time. In one chain e-mail I received a while ago, it was about Satan having a board meeting with his demonic spirits and they were discussing how to make Christians ineffective and one of them stated that if they could keep Christians busy with the cares of this world then they would become ineffective followers of the enemy [Jesus Christ]. If that is Satan's game plan, how well it works. Jesus speaks out against covetousness and complacement in the following parable:

> "And one of the company said unto him, Master, speak to my brother, that he divide the inheritance with me. 14 And he said unto him, Man, who made me a judge or a divider over you? 15 And he said unto them, Take heed, and beware of covetousness: for a man's life consisteth not in the abundance of the things which he possesseth. 16 And he spake a parable unto them, saying, The ground of a certain rich man brought forth plentifully: 17 And he thought within himself, saying, What shall I do, because I have no room where to bestow my fruits? 18 And he

said, This will I do: I will pull down my barns, and build greater; and there will I bestow all my fruits and my goods. 19 And I will say to my soul, Soul, thou hast much goods laid up for many years; take thine ease, eat, drink, and be merry. 20 But God said unto him, Thou fool, this night thy soul shall be required of thee: then whose shall those things be, which thou hast provided? 21 So is he that layeth up treasure for himself, and is not rich toward God."

(Luke 12:13-21 KJV).

This parable is the opposite of a popular misconception in the world around us. As far as the world around us is concerned, a man's life *does* exist in the abundance of things he possesses, thus they try to amass more and more things to themselves. Jesus is declaring that you must be careful of covetousness because a man's life *does not* exist in the things he possesses. What then does a man's life consist of? It consists of relationships, which are more important than possessions. Our relationship with God is more important and more valuable than all of the possessions we can possibly acquire. It is tragic that so many men, who are trapped in covetousness because of their greed, have alienated themselves from any meaningful relationships. Too many families have been broken because the husband was so driven by his desire to get ahead that he neglected his relationship with his family at home. Many executives and lesser blue-collar men have driven themselves to heart attacks. Heart attacks are a very common ailment among executives. Unfortunately, this addiction is not limited to men, but also women who drive themselves until they destroy their health. Covetousness is something that can hardly ever be satisfied. It will continue to drive a person harder and harder (like a sports figure who comes out of retirement, not so much for the money, but to relive the glory) until it destroys those things that are most important. Life consists of relationships.

Interestingly enough is the contrast between the man's opinion of himself and God's opinion of him. His opinion of himself was 'I got it made.' God's opinion of him was 'thy fool'. As Jesus was speaking, the man was still in the dream state of his plan, he had not yet built the bigger barns. His plan was—as soon as he had built bigger barns and filled them…to kick back, eat, drink, and be merry. The problem is--he never arrived at that point. When we die, there is no more opportunity to store up treasures for ourselves. This one life here on earth is our only opportunity to lay up for ourselves much treasure in heaven by being in God's Will and walking in God's Purpose for our life.

If he had not died that night and continued to live and gone ahead and torn down his barns and built bigger ones, and filled them, he still would not have been satisfied. If covetousness is your god (the spirit that's ruling you) then that spirit is not going to just up and depart on its own… it's a bondage Satan will keep you in for life. The man probably would never have said…I have enough. I believe that you and I have been around long enough to witness this for ourselves in people and loved ones around us. I remember a question was asked of J. D. Rockefeller, 'how much is enough'—and his reply was—'just a little bit more.' It's like an alcoholic or drug addict: they may sincerely want to quit, but the substance addiction, combined with a controlling demonic spirit will not let that happen anytime soon. So it is, a tragic loss for the man or woman who lays up treasures for themselves and is not rich toward God. Jesus says to you and I... do not be covetous. As with this man, we rarely consider the afterlife: all we know is that we want to go to heaven when we die. Whatever your reason for not wanting to go to *Hell*, the question we have to ask ourselves is—is there more to the afterlife than what we may have heard or read?

Listen to what God said to the Prophet Zechariah (my namesake) concerning Joshua the High Priest in the afterlife:

> "Thus saith the LORD of hosts; If thou wilt walk in my ways, and if thou wilt keep my charge, then thou shalt also judge my house, and shalt also keep my courts, and I will give thee places to walk among these that stand by."
>
> (Zech 3:7 KJV).

If I use my sanctified imagination (and that could be dangerous) in thinking of places to walk in the heavenlies, I can see myself having breakfast on Mars, lunch on Pluto, dinner in another galaxy, and getting back in time for worship service.

Another reason you might want to make a Vow of Commitment is for inoculation against a collaborative effort of demonic forces attempting to cause you to miss out on ministry opportunity for the lord and/or at least be miserable in performing it. Always remember, the joy of the Lord is your strength! Jesus reminds us in the Book of John:

"Herein is my Father glorified, that ye bear much fruit; so shall ye be my disciples."

(John 15:8 KJV).

I find it so easy for us, as believers, to be talked out of doing things by demonic forces (we wrestle not against flesh and blood) that if it wasn't for discernment, the church would be much weaker than it already is. The enemy is very good at using our flesh and state of mind against us. It is not until we soul search why we're doing whatever it is we have committed to doing do we arrive at the proper conclusion, which is to be an available vessel to our Lord and Savior. The enemy plays tricks with our minds and convince us that we're too tired today to minister, or it's too hot/cold outside, or next week will be better, etc. I remember back in January of 2007, I was driving home and debating witnessing door-to-door. I was thinking that people would not respond because of the cold weather... just then, I spotted two Mormons riding their bicycles through the neighborhood and sharing their faith. Deacon V. Taylor, Sis P. Emanuel, and I go to the prison on Tuesday evenings and teach Bible Study from 7-9 P.M. When it's time to change and get ready, it seems like I am the most tired person in the world around 6 P.M. Sometimes I reason with myself that Deacon Taylor can handle it, he will understand that I was too tired to make it. Then I realize that it is only Satan trying to steal my joy. If I had continued to lie on the couch and missed Bible Study, the rest of the evening I would be asking for God's forgiveness. Also, I would have to explain to Deacon Taylor and the men at the prison who come out faithfully why I did not show up. What a sorry excuse, 'I was too tired' *or* 'I fell asleep' on the one night of the week that we meet at the prison to have Bible Study.

When I recognize that it is just Satan doing what he does best, I move out and accomplish the mission. What an awesome time we have at the prison on Tuesday evenings! Those men come hungry. They realize that God has them in a place where He can get their undivided attention. Many of them thank God that they are in prison instead of dead or homeless on the streets. Our job as servants of the Most High God is to plant the seed and not judge:

> "For all have sinned and fallen short of the Glory of God."
>
> *(Roman* 3:23 KJV*).*

I would like to lift out a prayer God committed to from an ordinary person, just like you and I in the Book of 2 Chronicles:

> "And Jabez was more honoured than his brethren; and his mother called his name Jabez, saying, Because I bore him with pain. ¹⁰ And Jabez called on the God of Israel saying, Oh that thou wouldest richly bless me, and enlarge my border, and that thy hand might be with me, and that thou wouldest keep me from evil, that it may not grieve me! And God brought about what he had requested."
>
> (1 Chronicles 4:9-10 KJV).

In the midst of a genealogy, the Holy Spirit paused and related to us a special prayer that pleased God. The Prayer of Jabez primarily was an unselfish prayer. He asked for no specific thing. He concluded that whatever God blessed him with would suffice. There is no mention of his employment which he asked God to enlarge, just a desire to do more for God with what he had. He cried out to God to enlarge his territory that he may draw others unto Him [God]. His cry was not a selfish one, but one that would bless God and others. Jabez cried out *'Ohhhhhhh'* (you have to put some emotion in it) that you would bless me to be a blessing! God committed to Jabez's prayer request because it pleased God. I believe this vow you make from your heart will please the heart of God as well because it is purely voluntary.

ADULT COMMITMENT:

Your commitment should be something that is completely out of your normal routine. Something that will require a sacrifice of your time, gifts, and talents. This may involve leading a Bible Study in a prison or a Bible Study at a Shelter for Battered Women, or a Bible Study at a Homeless Shelter. It may involve a weekly visit to a Nursing Home and having a personal, one-on-one, Bible Study. It may even involve Bible Study at someone's bedside in or out of the hospital.

DOOR KNOCKING

This is the ministry I believe will be your greatest challenge. If you read the Book of Luke, Chapter 16, verses 19-31, you will find a story about the reality of 'Hell'. God [Jesus Christ] is the only person in the Bible to describe the activities of Hell. Combine this teaching with the Apostle Paul's teaching to the Corinthians about unbelievers being blinded by the god of this world [Satan] and you will get a whole new perspective on ministry.

> "In whom the god of this world hath blinded the minds of them which believe not, lest the light of the glorious gospel of Christ, who is the image of God, should shine unto them."
>
> (2 Cor 4:4 KJV).

I believe your vow will do the most good going from door to door in your community, offering Christ to a dying world. The rejection is tremendous. Nevertheless, your vow is not about you, it is about your desire to do more to serve God.

> "For God so loved the world, that he gave his only begotten Son, that whosoever believeth in him should not perish, but have everlasting life"
>
> (John 3:16 KJV).

Door knocking will open your eyes to the extent of the blindness the god of this world [Satan] has accomplished. The temperature outside may not be comfortable and Satan will surely use that against you. I have struggled many days with going out in the heat of the evening (El Paso, TX desert heat) and door knocking on doors verses going straight home in the evenings, but I knew and expected this kind of demonic warfare and in my heart, I know I want to do my part in fulfilling the Great Commission.

Be prayed up. Try not to go alone. Take your Pastor's business cards and other church materials that has your churches address and phone numbers on it. Some of the people you meet will accept Christ, but may not want to come to your church right away (if at all) so make sure you get their name, phone number(s) (home and cell), and their address so that you can follow up. I attended a 90% African American church and most of the people I have led to Christ are Hispanic and will not attend our church. They still need to be baptized. Discuss those procedures with your pastor. Sacrifice and Obedience is the key. You may not see the fruit of the seeds you planted, but great is your reward in heaven. Concerning rewards, Jesus said:

> "Do not store up for yourselves treasures on earth, where moth and rust destroy, and where thieves break in and steal. But store up for yourselves treasures in heaven, where moth and rust do not destroy, and where thieves do not break in and steal."
>
> (Matt 6:19-20 KJV).

The attitude in which anyone approaches ministry should be of sheer love. Whether God rewarded us or not, if whatever we do for God is not out of pure love, with no hidden agenda, then what we have done would have been in vain in the eyes of God. Yes, God wants the gospel to spread, but only with the right attitude. If ministry becomes a burden to anyone, they should get out of ministry and do something else. Ministry is not a burden when you have a right relationship with God. Therefore, this adventure of partaking of the Vow of Commitment is a private spiritual reward from God Himself. *Do Not* look to others for a pat on the back, *Do Not* look to others for a shoulder to cry on. In your private devotion time, gain strength in the Lord. Cry on His shoulders:

> "This book of the law shall not depart out of thy mouth; but thou shalt meditate therein day and night, that thou mayest observe to do according to all that is written therein: for then thou shalt make thy way prosperous, and then thou shalt have good success. Have not I commanded thee? Be strong and of a good courage; be not afraid, neither be thou dismayed: for the LORD thy God is with thee whithersoever thou goest."
>
> (Joshua 1:8-9 KJV).

PRISON MINISTRY

This is the area to which I have been called. You first have to be cleared to enter the prison. This requires a background check. Simply call the prison and ask to speak to the chaplain. Make an appointment with him/her and ask for a volunteer application. Ask what ministry is needed most. It takes about two months for a background check to be completed before you can be cleared. After you have been cleared, you will have to attend an orientation at the prison to learn what the prison rules are for volunteers. In the meantime, try to join a prison ministry while your background investigation is being conducted. There may be people in your church who has loved ones in jail and all the inmates will need to do is put your name on their visiting list. Use the time of your Vow of Commitment, until you have been cleared to participate in an existing prison ministry or find out how and when you will be able to start your own. To me, there is nothing more rewarding than pioneering your own ministry. This requires the most trust in Christ to open doors for you and teaches you to wholly depend on Him. I'm reminded of the Apostle Paul who never went where the gospel had already been preached in:

"I have therefore whereof to boast in Christ Jesus in the things which pertain to God. 18 For I will not dare to speak anything of the things which Christ has not wrought by me, for the obedience of the nations, by word and deed, 19 in the power of signs and wonders, in the power of the Spirit of God; so that I, from Jerusalem, and in a circuit round to Illyricum, have fully preached the glad tidings of the Christ; 20 and so aiming to announce the glad tidings, not where Christ has been named, that I might not build upon another's foundation; 21 but according as it is written, To whom there was nothing told concerning him, they shall see; and they that have not heard shall understand."

(Romans 15:17-21 KJV)

NURSING HOME MINISTRY

Start by asking the program manager what the daily activities are of the tenants. Ask if it's okay for you to go room to room just to see if anyone would like visitation. As you go room-to-room, start a conversation by asking them how they are doing, how they are feeling, would they like some company, etc. Be prepared to listen to their life story. Be prepared to spend an hour or two with just one person.

Be genuinely interested in what they are saying, all the while listening to the Holy Spirit as He may have been preparing their hearts for you to share the Gospel with them (make sure you know how to lead someone to Christ, Romans 10:8-11). God may have them hanging on long enough for you to reach them with the good news of the Gospel of Jesus Christ. Continue visits with Sunday School lessons, listen to your Pastor's sermon with them, or read a couple of chapters of a good book with them. While reading, studying or listening, you come to a certain topic you can specifically relate to, share your personal experience with them. Chances are they will have their own experiences to relate also. You will be so surprised how the Holy Spirit can use you to minister to a complete stranger if you just step out in faith. Before returning, find out what day is the best day and time to visit them.

HOSPITAL MINISTRY

For those who love to pray. This ministry offers the most acceptance to the gospel. However, that doesn't mean that you specifically use this as an open door to share the gospel. Your primary mission is to offer comfort through prayer. They will see you as a person who can get a message through to God. They may have no Jesus at all or they may be in a '*back slidden*' state. They may only need reassuring that God loves them unconditionally. I guarantee you the Holy Spirit will open up a door for you to share the gospel at just the right time. Wait on the Holy Spirit. As you communicate with them, you will be able to tell what kind (if any) of relationship they have with Christ. Ask them what their specific prayer requests are. Let them know that you will ask your church to be praying for them also.

On your second visit, try to bring a small gift (a $3-5 plant, gift, food, etc...). The more personal you are, the more open they will become. Once Jesus healed the people, they were receptive to the gospel. Your prayer is the first step in the spiritual healing that they need. Take some 'anointing oil' with you. Some churches do not use the oil; I do because we're told to do so:

> "Is any one of you sick? He should call the elders of the church to pray over him and anoint him with oil in the name of the LORD. 15And the prayer offered in faith will make the sick person well; the LORD will raise him up. If he has sinned, he will be forgiven."
>
> (James 5:14-15 KJV).

Try not to go alone on the first visit. Depending on the gender, the second visit can be alone (males visiting males and females visiting females).

YOUTH COMMITMENT: DOOR KNOCKING

For the young and the brave. If possible, send out a minimum of 3 teens per group door-to-door on Saturday mornings followed by a specific activity later on the same day. Knock on the door and introduce yourself, the church you represent, and your purpose. Your purpose is to invite the teens in the neighborhood to participate in your church's Youth activities. Some activities can be conducted at your neighborhood recreation center, especially if it has a swimming pool. The goal, however, is to get them used to coming to church.

YOUTH BIBLE STUDY

Youth Bible Study should be separate from Adult Bible Study. It can be done at someone's home in their backyard, or at the church. Preferably at your church to get them used to coming to church. It can be done at the same time as Adult Bible Study, but in a different location of the church. Bible study for youth is most effective following some type of fun organized sport like volleyball. A sport where no one is likely to get hurt and all can participate.

FRIDAY NIGHT MOVIE

Friday or Saturday afternoon. Have lots of popcorn and drinks. Watch only appropriate material and find the biblical morals displayed in the characters. Point out the weakness of the characters and how the Bible addresses those weaknesses. Point out the strengths of the characters and how society rewards those strengths. Point out the relationships the characters has with or without God and how God blesses our relationship with Him. Encourage the youth that they too can achieve the same success in life no matter what their present situation or living condition is because their Heavenly Father has no respect-a-person. Point out that all that is required of them is a trusting relationship with Jesus. Be aware that children will tell everything that is going on in their homes with their parents and siblings. Make sure a mature Christian adult is present with biblical answers for their unique situation. Never allow the other kids to laugh and make fun of their situation. Control the environment. Everyone should be able to share without the fear of being laughed at or mocked.

It is imperative that the atmosphere be one of Christian learning and sharing.

OPEN MIC NIGHT

At Sun City Christian Fellowship Baptist Church, every Friday evening, the youth ministers host an 'Open Mic Night' where the youth may read a poem they wrote, or sing along to their favorite song, or a *rap* song they wrote for Jesus, etc. Of course, some of them will be embarrassed at first, but this is where the Youth Ministers come into play and begin to build up their courage and self-esteem. In addition, the other youths also encourage them to go up to the mic and no matter how good or bad they do, all are cheered and given high-five's after they leave the mic and head back to their seat. I remember my daughter Destinee went up for the first time to the mic and read a poem that she wrote during a sleep over at the 'Adventure Zone,' here in El Paso, TX. Our church rented the whole facility and the youth played games all night long and brought their sleeping bags. I asked the ministers and one of the minister's wife, Sis Y. Hallback, to encourage my daughter to read her poem. Eventually she did and I believe that I was more excited than she was when she had finished. This is an inexpensive way to reach the youth in your neighborhood.

BACKYARD BARBEQUE/PICNIC

Another way that may be a little bit more expensive would be to have a backyard barbeque (hotdogs and hamburgers) or picnic (sandwiches and chips) with randomly picked volleyball teams, making sure everyone gets picked and a chance to play. Allow time for a short message by a Youth Pastor or Leader. Remember, this is for the youth, by the youth, but with adult supervision. Your ultimate goal is to get the youth to attend your church regularly.

Chapter 6

EXPECT THE UNEXPECTED

"Finally, be strong in the LORD and in his mighty power. Put on the full armor of God so that you can take your stand against the devil's schemes. For our struggle is not against flesh and blood, but against the rulers, against the authorities, against the powers of this dark world and against the spiritual forces of evil in the heavenly realms."

(Eph 6:10-12 NKJV).

USURPED AUTHORITY

When God created the world and placed man upon it, God gave man dominion over it.

"26 And God said, Let us make man in our image, after our likeness: and let them have dominion over the fish of the sea, and over the fowl of the air, and over the cattle, and over all the earth, and over every creeping thing that creepeth upon the earth. 27 So God created man in his own image, in the image of God created he him; male and female created he them. 28 And God blessed them, and God said unto them, Be fruitful, and multiply, and replenish the earth, and subdue it: and have dominion over the fish of the sea, and over the fowl of the air, and over every living thing that moveth upon the earth."

(*Gen* 1:26-28 KJV).

Man [Adam], in the Garden of Eden, gave it unto Satan. Too often we do not see the spiritual implications of our actions. This is what God sees and if we would just be obedient to the words of God, we can avoid so many physical normalities resulting from unseen spiritual implications. For instance, Satan did not tell Adam and Eve that dominion over the earth would pass from Adam to himself. This dominion is not physical, but spiritual. Nor did Satan tell Adam and Eve that they would certainly die spiritually (separation from God). We see today the disastrous consequences of Satan's rule. The wars, the sufferings, the homicides, child abuse—all of these things are the consequence of Satan's rule. When we pray the model prayer Jesus gave to His disciples, we pray, 'Thy kingdom come, Thy will be done on earth as it is in heaven'—but we do not yet see God's will being done on earth. In the Book of Hebrews we read that 'God hath put all things into subjection unto Jesus, but we do not yet see all things in subjection unto Him (Hebrews 2:8). In fact, we are still in a world in rebellion against God and we still see the fruit of that rebellion in this nation in which we live. One day, by the grace of God we will live in a world that God intended. There is a marvelous description of that world in the Old Testament where the lion will lie down with the lamb (back to a vegetarian society), and the blind shall behold the glory of our Lord (no physical maladies) for the former things will be passed away and all things will become new and there will be no suffering for we will see the world in harmony with God as God intended and wants the world to be:

"And there shall come forth a rod out of the stem of Jesse, and a Branch shall grow out of his roots: 2 And the spirit of the LORD shall rest upon him, the spirit of wisdom and understanding, the spirit of counsel and might, the spirit of knowledge and of the fear of the LORD; 3 And shall make him of quick understanding in the fear of the LORD: and he shall not judge after the sight of his eyes, neither reprove after the hearing of his ears: 4 But with righteousness shall he judge the poor, and reprove with equity for the meek of the earth: and he shall smite the earth with the rod of his mouth, and with the breath of his lips shall he slay the wicked. 5 And righteousness shall be the girdle of his loins, and faithfulness the girdle of his reins. 6 The wolf also shall dwell with the lamb, and the leopard shall lie down with the kid; and the calf and the young lion and the fatling together; and a little child shall lead them. 7 And the cow and the bear shall feed; their young ones shall lie down together: and the lion shall eat straw like the ox. 8 And the sucking child shall play on the hole of the asp, and the weaned child shall put his hand on the cockatrice' den. 9 They shall not hurt nor destroy in all my holy mountain: for the earth shall be full of the knowledge of the LORD, as the waters cover the sea."

(Isaiah 11:1-9 KJV).

At the present moment we see a world in rebellion and we see men under Satan's control. The Bible tells us that Satan has taken them captive, even against their will:

> "Flee also youthful lusts: but follow righteousness, faith, charity, peace, with them that call on the LORD out of a pure heart. 23 But foolish and unlearned questions avoid, knowing that they do gender strifes. 24 And the servant of the LORD must not strive; but be gentle unto all men, apt to teach, patient, 25 In meekness instructing those that oppose themselves; if God peradventure will give them repentance to the acknowledging of the truth; 26 And that they may recover themselves out of the snare of the devil, who are taken captive by him at his will."
>
> (2 Tim 2:22-26 KJV).

The Apostle Paul tells us that the God of this world has blinded their eyes that they cannot see the truth! There are men today who cannot see the truth, they are bound by Satan's power, they are blinded by him:

> "But if our gospel be hid, it is hid to them that are lost: 4 In whom the god of this world hath blinded the minds of them which believe not, lest the light of the glorious gospel of Christ, who is the image of God, should shine unto them."
>
> (2 Cor 4:3-4 KJV).

We see men in bondage to corruption and in bondage to sin. We see it holding men in its power and we have seen the vain, futile struggle of man to try and free himself from that power of darkness. Now, the Holy Spirit is reproving the world of sin and of righteousness and of judgment because the prince of this world was judged at the cross (John 16:7-11). What that means is that you don't have to be under Satan's power. You don't have to be under the bondage of corruption. The Apostle John teaches us that this is one of the reasons for Jesus' first coming:

> "He that committeth sin is of the devil; for the devil sinneth from the beginning. For this purpose the Son of God was manifested, that he might destroy the works of the devil."
>
> (1 John 3:8 KJV).

Jesus' first coming in the flesh was physical indeed, but more centered on the spiritual welfare of man than anything else. Case in point, the paraplegic was let down through the roof by his friends that Jesus might heal him (Mark 2:1-5). The first thing Jesus did was heal his spiritual condition. Jesus' second coming will be in his 'glorified' body, but physically ruling and reining on earth for 1000 years, known as the Millennial Rein of Christ. The second thing Jesus did was heal his physical body,; this coincides with the type of life that will be realized during the Millennial Rein of Christ when there will be no physical maladies. The good news is— because of the cross of Jesus Christ and His victory over Satan there at the cross, His victory became our victory. Through the power of Jesus Christ, we can have complete victory and power over the world, the flesh, and the devil. You do not have to be under Satan's power. Actually, what Satan holds today, he holds by what is called 'usurped' power and authority.

In other words, the power Satan has is not really his—he usurps it. When God rejected Saul from being the King over Israel because of his disobedience, God sent and said to Samuel 'how long are you going to grieve for Saul, seeing I have rejected him. Go down to the house of Jesse and anoint one of his sons to be the king over Israel' (1 Samuel 16:1). So Samuel snuck down to the house of Jesse for fear of Saul and he said to Jesse, 'would you bring your sons before me' and the first son Eliab came in, big, tall, strong and handsome and Samuel thought that surly this is the one God has chosen for the king but God said to Samuel, 'don't look on the outward appearance for I don't look on the outward appearance, I look on the heart.' Eliab's not the one. So, one by one, the sons of Jesse walked in and marched by Samuel and each one the Lord said–no. Finally, Samuel turned to Jesse and asked, 'don't you have any other sons? Yea, I have one more, he's just a kid out watching the sheep. Well, call him in; and when David came in, this ruddy little kid, the Lord said to Samuel–that's the one. Samuel took his oil and he poured it over David's head and anointed him as king over Israel.

Now, I said all of that to say this, as far as God was concerned David was the King. God anointed him as king; however, Saul did not want to give up his position as king and he wanted one of his sons [Jonathan] to succeed him as king. We read in the next few chapters how that Saul did his best to kill David–and to hang onto the kingdom that God had taken away. Samuel's condemnation to Saul was 'because you had rejected God from ruling over you, God has rejected you from ruling over the kingdom.' However, Saul did his best by force to hold onto that which God had taken away. The exact same thing Satan is doing today, but Satan was not installed as the god of this world, it is a position that he has taken by deception and by force. Now, the same is true today in the lives of people. Jesus has died on the cross to redeem the world from Satan, but Satan still holds people under his power by his 'usurped' power, it is no longer legally, rightfully his. Jesus has purchased all who will believe in Him by His blood. Therefore, we can enter into that victory of Jesus over Satan at the cross and we can also lay claim to lives that Satan is holding. We can take them from the captivity of the enemy who has taken them captive by bring them before the Lord in prayer–case by case. We can pray, 'Lord, I claim the power of Jesus Christ and His victory over the power of Satan that is holding them and blinding them (whoever it is you are praying for). Lord, deliver them from the power of the enemy and from the blindness.' It is very important to know that we cannot save them through our prayers, but we can at least bring them before God that He might offer to them the freedom of choice.

People of the world today think that they are a 'free moral agent' and have the right to choose how they want to live their life. However, there is no way you can say of a sinner that he is a free moral agent because he is the most bound person in the universe. In his or her mind, physically speaking, they believe they are free to make their own choices, but their eyes are blind and they are being held captive by the power of Satan. He or she is not a free moral agent–they are a slave! They are under the power of the enemy–but through prayer, we can make them a free moral agent. Through prayer, we can break the bondage of Satan's power and through prayer, we can open their eyes to the truth. At that point, being a free moral agent, he or she can then choose without the oppressive work of Satan blinding their eyes and twisting and perverting their logic. With this in mind, we can clearly see that the power of prayer toward the sinner is that of setting them free from this bondage of Satan, the same bondage we were set free from. Satan has no legal rights over them anymore and we can claim the victory for Christ—life, after life, after life—setting them free from the power of darkness.

FEAR

The enemy uses fear against us. The fear of failure, the fear of rejection, the fear of what people might say about us. He gets us to the point where we have failed in our minds before we even begin. The mere possibility of success is never realized because the project never gets off the ground. God drops it in our spirit, but we let the devil talk us out of it. Instead of just sitting around wondering if God is in the midst of whatever endeavor you're planning to undertake—just go for it! If doors do not open…God's not in it. If doors open…God's in it. Waiting to hear God speak to you may not happen until you get to heaven. Step out on faith! Moses sent ten spies to spy out the Promised Land and two came back with a good report, but the other eight came back with fear in their hearts and *their* fear caused the Israel-ites to wander for forty years in the wilderness (one year for each day the spies were spying out the land). This evil report angered the Lord because they should've had more faith… after all, had not God departed the Red Sea for them to go across on? I connect the fear these eight fearful men displayed to the demonic spirits who whisper in our spiritual ears, 24/7, telling us what we cannot do. Fear brings unbelief, and that unbelief will rob you of that which God has already been made available for you and is waiting to be claimed—just sitting on a shelf and waiting for you to pick it up—just waiting—and waiting—and waiting. God puts all things that edify the Body of Christ within our reach—not our lap! Our *faith* will put it in our lap.

WILDERNESS JOURNEY

The wilderness experience is necessary for faith. There were two routes the Israelites could have taken: the short route and the long route. The short route from Mt. Horeb to the Promised Land was 11 days (Deut 1:2). The long route from Mt. Horeb to the Promised Land was 40 years. God led them through the short route first. The Israelites were right at the door of the Promised Land and all they had to do was go in and possess it! God had already promised to drive out the inhabitants from before them. They were to walk in and take the land—*but*—because they allowed *fear* instead of *faith* to dominate their hearts... they failed to go into the Promised Land. For the next forty years, God would lead them, trial by trial, building up their faith, through the wilderness.

There are seven "I Will" God uses in the Book of Exodus, Chapter 6. Israel's typical history typifies the Child of God coming out of bondage to the enemy. All through the Bible, Egypt represents bondage to sin and Babylon represents idolatry. Once they believed and followed Moses, God led them through the Red Sea, which represents baptism. Once we receive Jesus Christ as our Lord and Savior (Moses was a *type* of Christ), we are to be baptized in the name of the Father, and of the Son, and of the Holy Ghost. We are baptized in the name of the Trinity with the full power of the trinity available to the believer who allows God to work in their life by faith and service to God. In other words, when we count the cost and become a disciple of Jesus Christ, we become a channel for which God can flow through to accomplish *His will* in a lost world. It is at this point in our life, when we are ready to go where God says go and do what God says do, do we have all the fullness of the Godhead working within us to be a vessel unto God (John 14:23). When the Israelites went through the Red Sea, they were baptized into a new relationship of faith with God in the wilderness. God's intentions were to make them a *light* to the nations around them that through them, the nations might come to know the true and living God and have a relationship with Him. This is God's intentions for the church today. Because no one had seen God, the gentile nations made themselves gods (little g) which they could see and bow down and worship. One major problem with that is that the hands of man which made the god was greater than the god because man was the creator, thus they bowed down and prayed to a god that was less than they who made them.

For this reason (and many others), God sent Jesus Christ, the express image of Himself, into the world that we might know Him. We now know what God looks like. Jesus told Phillip, "If you have seen Me, you have seen the Father" (John 14:8-9, *emphasis mine*).

Baptism represents the death of the old sin nature and the newness of life born of the Holy Spirit (Jesus was born of the Holy Spirit in the Virgin Mary). Baptism represents death of the old life in bondage to sin and newness of life in the Promised Land. A land flowing with *milk* and *honey;* a life of richness and fullness in Jesus Christ. We can take these *I wills* of God given to Israel and we can apply them to our own lives which God is promising to deliver us. He has promised to deliver us from the heavy burdens of a satanic world system, from the bondage of our flesh to the things of this world, resulting in the old life of sin and separation from God. *I will* redeem you, *I will* take you for a people, *I will* be to you a God, and *I will* bring you into the fullness of that to which *I have* promised. This is the process of salvation--switching allegiance from a cruel taskmaster [Satan], to a faithful and loving God [Jehovah].

The Israelites never gained anything of permanent value while wondering in the wilderness (except God's chastisement which turned their hearts back to God). It is not until they entered into the Promised Land did they *possess their possessions*. Listen to what God said about Caleb in vs24:

> "But as truly as I live, all the earth shall be filled with the glory of the LORD. 22 Because all those men which have seen my glory, and my miracles, which I did in Egypt and in the wilderness, and have tempted me now these ten times, and have not hearkened to my voice; 23 Surely they shall not see the land which I sware unto their fathers, neither shall any of them that provoked me see it: 24 But my

servant Caleb, because he had another spirit with him, and hath followed me fully, him will I bring into the land whereinto he went; and his seed shall possess it."

(Num 14:21-24 KJV)

Another kind of spirit was in Caleb. What kind of spirit?

"For God hath not given us the spirit of fear; but of power, and of love, and of a sound mind."

(2 Tim 1:7 KJV).

TRAGEDY

Here is the tragedy of the church today. God has led us to the fulfilled life, a life full of blessings in Jesus Christ. However, there are so many Christians who have failed to enter into the full, rich life that God wants for His children. Christians wandering through the wilderness are living a life of *endurance* instead of a life of *enjoyment*. Their life is one continuous battle with the flesh... just wandering in the wilderness. I wandered for seventeen years. The wilderness represents the normal growth of the believer. The Promised Land represents the full life we can have in Christ. As God went ahead of the Israelites as a pillar of cloud by day and a pillar of fire by night (even the place the Israelites camped is the spot God had picked out) so has Christ paved the way for each believer to live a life of victory, fullness of joy, and spiritual blessings. The tragedy of many believers is their holding on to the things of the world, the things that are familiar to them. The elder generation of Israelites who did not believe as Caleb and Joshua did, they did not enter the Promised Land because of fear and a lack of faith. They died in the wilderness. The same goes for many believers in the world today (some of whom maybe in our own family) who may never enter into the Promised Land because they are blinded by the *god* of this world [Satan] and they love their sin.

The writer of the Hebrew's teaches us:

> "But without faith it is impossible to please him: for he that cometh to God must believe that he is, and that he is a rewarder of them that diligently seek him."
>
> (Heb 11:6 KJV).

EXPECT TO BE ATTACKED

Satan would not be Satan if he did not attack you. In war there will be casualties. There will be victories and there will be defeats. Can we really expect to fight against Satan's kingdom and not expect him to fight back? Whether you take the *Vow of Commitment* or not, just being a Christian qualifies you for an attack by the enemy of your soul. You have to be strong in the Lord no matter what you decide to do. As we walk this Christian journey, the greater the anointing God gives us, the greater the attack. Satan does not want to see people saved nor comforted. In the Book of Isaiah, Satan is described as an evil prison warden who does not lose his prisoners:

> "How art thou fallen from heaven, O Lucifer, son of the morning! how art thou cut down to the ground, which didst weaken the nations! 13For thou hast said in thine heart, I will ascend into heaven, I will exalt

my throne above the stars of God: I will sit also upon the mount of the congregation, in the sides of the north: ¹⁴I will ascend above the heights of the clouds; I will be like the most High. ¹⁵Yet thou shalt be brought down to hell, to the sides of the pit. ¹⁶They that see thee shall narrowly look upon thee, and consider thee, saying, Is this the man that made the earth to tremble, that did shake kingdoms; ¹⁷That made the world as a wilderness, and destroyed the cities thereof; that opened not the house of his prisoners."

(Isaiah 14:12-17 KJV).

God, in His infinite wisdom has chosen to work through mankind to bring about His purpose for the human race. Since God has chosen to work through man, so must Satan work through man to accomplish his purpose. Satan has no intentions of letting any believer in Christ develop an intimate relationship with God without his interference. Remember, the thief [Satan] comes but to steal, kill, and destroy. The people we witness to are in a spiritual prison and we have the keys to the prison doors. It wasn't too long ago that we too were in bondage to Satan until someone offered us the keys to free ourselves. The Apostle Paul speaks of his mission from Jesus to the Gentiles at his trial defense:

"Whereupon as I went to Damascus with authority and commission from the chief priests, 13 At midday, O king, I saw in the way a light from heaven, above the brightness of the sun, shining round about me and them which journeyed with me. 14 And when we were all fallen to the earth, I heard a voice speaking unto me, and saying in the Hebrew tongue, Saul,

Saul, why persecutest thou me? it is hard for thee to kick against the pricks. 15 And I said, Who art thou, LORD? And he said, I am Jesus whom thou persecutest. 16 But rise, and stand upon thy feet: for I have appeared unto thee for this purpose, to make thee a minister and a witness both of these things which thou hast seen, and of those things in the which I will appear unto thee; 17 Delivering thee from the people, and from the Gentiles, unto whom now I send thee, 18 To open their eyes, and to turn them from darkness to light, and from the power of Satan unto God, that they may receive forgiveness of sins, and inheritance among them which are sanctified by faith that is in me."

(Acts 26:12-18 KJV)

There are none so blind as those who *will not* see and none so blind as those *who cannot* see. Here Paul speaks of those who cannot see. The God of this world has blinded their eyes that they cannot see, lest the glorious light of the gospel of Jesus Christ should shine on them and they turn from him to Christ. Our world is in spiritual darkness and we can testify to it by listening to the news everyday. Jesus said 'I am the light of the world, he that follows after me will not walk in darkness, but will have the light of life.' Paul's mission from the Lord was two parts: 1) to open their spiritual eyes... God no longer wanted them to be spiritually blinded, and 2) to deliver them from the power of Satan to God:

"But if our gospel be hid, it is hid to them that are lost: 4 In whom the god of this world hath blinded the minds of them which believe not, lest the light of the glorious gospel of Christ, who is the image of God, should shine unto them."

(2 Cor 4:3-4 KJV)

"He that committeth sin is of the devil; for the devil sinneth from the beginning. For this purpose the Son of God was manifested, that he might destroy the works of the devil."

(1 John 3:8 KJV)

God has no intention of saving this wicked flesh that Satan manipulates almost unhindered throughout the world! As committed believers in Jesus Christ, we are to overcome Satan with the Blood of the Lamb, the Word of our Testimony, and we are *not* to love our life unto death (Rev 12:11). Our witness is for Christ, the foundation of our faith. It is His shed blood on the cross which we preach. His shed blood on the cross for the sins of the world enables us to willingly defend the faith and give our life as a ransom to the lost. By this we acknowledge and identify with a righteous God who died for an unrighteous people that we might have a right to the Tree of Life.

FIGHT, FIGHT, FIGHT

"Finally, my brethren, be strong in the LORD, and in the power of his might. 11 Put on the whole armour of God, that ye may be able to stand against the wiles of the devil. 12 For we wrestle not against flesh and blood, but against principalities, against powers, against the rulers of the darkness of this world, against spiritual wickedness in high places. 13 Wherefore take unto you the whole armour of

God, that ye may be able to withstand in the evil day, and having done all, to stand. 14 Stand therefore, having your loins girt about with truth, and having on the breastplate of righteousness; 15 And your feet shod with the preparation of the gospel of peace; 16 Above all, taking the shield of faith, wherewith ye shall be able to quench all the fiery darts of the wicked. 17 And take the helmet of salvation, and the sword of the Spirit, which is the word of God: 18 Praying always with all prayer and supplication in the Spirit, and watching thereunto with all perseverance and supplication for all saints."

(Eph 6:10-18 KJV)

Fight my brothers and sisters in Christ, against all ungodliness; for in doing so, we fight against all the forces of Satan who is *focused* and *determined* to have all mankind worship him as god (Is 14:12-14). How can we do any less? Too many believers leave home every morning butt naked... wearing nothing but the man-made clothes on our backs. We react to situations in the physical and not the spiritual. For this reason, many believers end up assimilated back into the ways of the world. God accused the Israelites of stealing, murder, adultery, swearing falsely, and burning incense unto Baal, and walking after other God's whom they did not know... and afterwards, they come into His temple to worship Him (Jere 7:9-11). What an oxymoron!... attempting to serve two masters: a fallen angel and a living God. Satan (a fallen angel), through his Egyptian servants, put the Israelites in slavery in Egypt. Jehovah (God), through his servant Moses, delivered them from slavery in Egypt. The people we fight for

are blinded and cannot see. We see their final destina-
tion. We were on our way there. Now…through the
power of the Holy Spirit, we are a life jacket to those
who will receive Jesus Christ as their Lord and Savior
(Luke 16:19-31).

Chapter 7

REWARDS

"For we must all appear before the judgment seat of Christ; that every one may receive the things done in his body, according to that he hath done, whether it be good or bad"

(2 Cor 5:10 KJV).

Question... The day you die and stand before Christ at the 'Believers' judgment, will you be looking forward to the judgment–or–will you be ashamed?

So many people are ignorant of the Believers Judgment that they merely go to church out of tradition. Shall *you* hear *'Well done my good and faithful servant'...* and if so, for what? What have you done for Christ lately? We will not be judged for our sins--past, present, or future... Jesus has died on the cross for those. However, we shall all give an account of how we lived our lives and what we did with the gospel of Jesus Christ since being saved. Did we live it, did we keep it to ourselves, and/or--did we share it?

Question... How old is your last testimony?

God has chosen to work through His creation (*You*

and I) to have *His* will done. God wants to bless us while we're here on this earth and reward us for serving Him in the afterlife. There are two judgments: 1) The Believers Judgment, and 2) the Un-Believers Judgment.

THE BELIEVERS JUDGMENT

"For other foundation can no man lay than that is laid, which is Jesus Christ. 12 Now if any man build upon this foundation gold, silver, precious stones, wood, hay, stubble; 13 Every man's work shall be made manifest: for the day shall declare it, because it shall be revealed by fire; and the fire shall try every man's work of what sort it is. 14 If any man's work abide which he hath built thereupon, he shall receive a reward. 15 If any man's work shall be burned, he shall suffer loss: but he himself shall be saved; yet so as by fire"

(1 Cor 3:11-15 KJV).

The foundation is Christ. Everything else is *Apostasy*. Apostasy is false teachings. This is a dogmatic statement. There is *no* other truth! This world of *relativism* in which we live is nothing more than satanic doctrine of demonic seducing spirits (1 Tim 4:1-2)! Relativism is believing *only* what you want to believe. It's a one-way ticket to Hell! The foundation is Christ. The fact that everyman's work shall be made manifest declares the purpose of God for our lives.

Question... What happens to wood, hay, and stubble when it goes through the fire? *It is burned up.* What happens to Gold, silver, and precious stones when it goes through the fire? *It is refined and made pure.*

The fact that he shall be saved confirms that we *Do Not* work for salvation, but for a reward. At this judgment, the Holy Spirit will bear witness with our spirit that we are true believers in Jesus Christ (Romans 8:16, *emphasis mine*). However, even after admittance into heaven and that believer having no works to show for Christ's dying on the cross for his sins; for all eternity he/she will have to live with the shame of not having any gifts to present God who shed His blood for them. *Me*ology prevailed in his/her life. They never wandered *out* of the wilderness into the Promised Land.

THE UNBELIEVERS JUDGMENT

"And I saw a great white throne, and him that sat on it, from whose face the earth and the heaven fled away; and there was found no place for them. 12 And I saw the dead, small and great, stand before God; and the books were opened: and another book was opened, which is the book of life: and the dead were judged out of those things which were written in the books, according to their works. 13 And the sea gave up the dead which were in it; and death and hell delivered up the dead which were in them: and they were judged every man according to their works. 14 And death and hell were cast into the lake of fire. This is the second death. 15 And whosoever was not found written in the book of life was cast into the lake of fire."

(Rev 20:11-15 KJV)

Jesus Christ is very clear about the desires of our Father in heaven for His children:

"Fear not, little flock; for it is your Father's good pleasure to give you the kingdom."

(Luke 12:32 kjv).

"Seek ye first the kingdom of God, and his righteousness; and all these things shall be added unto you."

(Matt 6:33 kjv).

What once pertained strictly to the Jews, now pertain to you and I through the *Spirit of Adoption*. I want to emphasize the fact that we do not work for salvation, but we work for a reward.

Question...have you ever applied for a particular job that you really wanted and was later told that you got the job?

When you went to work, did you expect to receive a paycheck? Did you expect to get a raise or a promotion? Sure you did! Similarly, you are working for a reward that will be waiting for you when you get to heaven. Though these rewards will be waiting for you when you get to heaven, there are spiritual gratifications that you will experience down here on earth in ministry with our Lord and Savior... Jesus Christ. These precious personal spiritual enjoyments consist of deeper levels of intimacy and trust in God. It includes, but not limited to, being able to see the lost through the eyes of God, going to the next level in *your* thinking, *your* praying, and *your* devotion time. Essentially, the only way to obtain the Mind of Christ and the Heart of God, is through ministry to the least, the left out, and the lonely. All through the Bible, God demonstrates his concerns for the downtrodden and oppressed of society. The widow, the orphan, the poor, and the stranger (alien/immigrant) were of particular concern to God (James 1:27). Satan comes to kill, steal, and destroy by any means necessary. By not knowing the mind of Satan, people fall victims to the schemes of others, addictions, and a host of other predicaments that put them in poverty situations. As believers, we are to have the *mind* of Christ and *heart* of God in protecting and preserving life:

> "Let this mind be in you, which was also in Christ Jesus: 6 Who, being in the form of God, thought it not robbery to be equal with God: 7 But made himself of no reputation, and took upon him the form of a servant, and was made in the likeness of men: 8 And being found in fashion as a man, he humbled himself, and became obedient unto death, even the death of the cross. 9 Wherefore God also hath highly exalted him, and given him a name which is above every name"
>
> (Phil 2:5-9 KJV).

We can clearly see the reward of Christ for service to the Father. He was rewarded 1) For being obedient to the Father and being made lower than the angels for the purposes of dying on the cross for our sins (as God he could not die), 2) For becoming a man because by man (Adam) fellowship was lost and by man must fellowship be gained, 3) For redeeming the title deed to the earth from Satan (handed over to him by Adam), and 4) For living a sinless life in complete obedience to the Father. We exercise our free will when we serve God. Jesus had free will and could have came down off the cross if He wanted, but He did only the will of the

Father. We also forget that the Father has *free will* and can choose to do whatever He wants. He can choose to answer our prayers or not. He has promised to hear our prayers, but not to give us whatever we want. Not all things are good for us. This is the same relationship we have with our own children. We give them everything they need to be successful, but not everything they want. The Apostle Paul wanted to be healed from his infirmity Satan inflicted him with, but Jesus said *no* to him—yet to the Leper...Jesus said *yes*. We must never forget that if we have freewill, then so does God. We ask according to His will.

Let's use our sanctified imagination for a minute. Let's look beyond the physical and into the spiritual. Let's look beyond life on earth and look at a particular activity that shall take place in heaven—the Marriage of the Lamb. A sanctified imagination is kind of like dreaming, like having an out of body experience even though we might be lying on our bed asleep. The terminology is a cliché, an explanation for attempting to see the invisible with *spiritual* eyes:

> "Let us be glad and rejoice, and give honour to him: for the marriage of the Lamb is come, and his wife hath made herself ready. 8 And to her was granted that she should be arrayed in fine linen, clean and white: for the fine linen is the righteousness of saints. 9 And he saith unto me, Write, Blessed are they which are called unto the marriage supper of the Lamb. And he saith unto me, These are the true sayings of God."
>
> (Rev 19:7-9 kjv)

I want you to picture three wedding gowns (for

you macho guy's, Christ is the only one with the robe (tuxedo) for we (male and female's) are His bride (the church); remember, we're in spiritual and not physical bodies in heaven. The *first* gown has no decorations whatsoever… just a plain white gown. The *second* gown has some stripes on the sleeve and around the waist… definitely prettier. The *third* gown is fully adorned with a veil, a hat, lace, ruffles, a train, and gloves up to the elbow. Now… which wedding gown would you want to wear on your wedding day? The third one… *right!* The wedding gown that's *laid out*… adorned with all the bells and whistles.

The *first* gown will be worn by those who are saved by grace through faith in Jesus Christ, but do nothing to advance the kingdom of God. These type of Christians blend in with the unbelievers, they still speak the language of the world and watch material full of profanity that is inappropriate for Christian believers, however, they do call themselves a Christian and acknowledge Jesus Christ as the one who died on the cross for their sins. I call them *Secret Service Christians.*

The *second* gown will be worn by those who attend church regularly and perhaps are an usher in the church or sing in the choir, or a leader in the church, but have not prioritized their life to really get to know God more intimately through daily Bible devotions and prayer. The First Lady of our church, First Lady A. Payton, describes them as *saved but not delivered.*

Then there are those who will wear the *third* gown (the one that is decked out). These are the who have prioritized their life around Jesus Christ. These are they who openly show their love for Christ and are not ashamed of the Gospel. These are they who are known by their co-workers as a Christian. These are they who meditate on the scriptures day and night (Psalms 1). These are they who, when called by God to be a missionary, leave the comforts of home and go minister around the world in third world countries. These are they who obtain Seminary Certificates of Completions and Seminary College Degrees in an effort to give God more to work with *in addition to* a secular education (thanks Dr. Ronald Bobo, www.westsidembc.org).

In a Nutshell, what the Vow of Commitment does is offer you the perfect opportunity to adorn your wedding gown before God calls you home. In case you did not know, all believers who make it through the fire in 1 Cor 3:11-15, shall attend the *Marriage Supper* of the Lamb. The Marriage Supper takes place here on earth after the Marriage of the Lamb in heaven. As with any wedding, the bride and groom leave the church and go the reception for dinner and dancing. The tradition is to ride in a limousine from the church to the reception. When we come in glory with Christ at His *second* coming, our limo will be the clouds (now that's riding in style). We will honeymoon with Christ for 1000 years. This will be the longest honeymoon in the history of mankind. The One Thousand Year Rein of Christ on the earth is known as the Millennial Rein of Christ. Right now, while we're still here on earth, we are not the 'Bride of Christ' but the 'Body of Christ'. After the believer's judgment, during the tribulation period, at the Marriage of the Lamb, Christ shall present to Himself a *'Bride'* without spot or wrinkle. So then... now that you know what you know... which gown shall you strive to wear to the wedding?

Chapter 8

THE VOW OF COMMITMENT

"And the LORD spake unto Moses, saying, 2 Speak unto the children of Israel, and say unto them, When either man or woman shall separate themselves to vow a vow of a Nazarite, to separate themselves unto the LORD: 3 He shall separate himself from wine and strong drink, and shall drink no vinegar of wine, or vinegar of strong drink, neither shall he drink any liquor of grapes, nor eat moist grapes, or dried. 4 All the days of his separation shall he eat nothing that is made of the vine tree, from the kernels even to the husk. 5 All the days of the vow of his separation there shall no rasor come upon his head: until the days be fulfilled, in the which he separateth himself unto the LORD, he shall be holy, and shall let the locks of the hair of his head grow. 6 All the days that he separateth himself unto the LORD he shall come at no dead body. 7 He shall not make himself unclean for his father, or for his mother, for his brother, or for his sister, when they die: because the consecration of his God is upon his head. 8 All the days of his separation he is holy unto the LORD"

(Num 6:1-8 KJV).

Vows were a voluntary promise to God to perform some service or do something pleasing to Him in return for some hoped benefits. A vow had to be spoken to be binding. Israelites made special vows by promising or dedicating persons, animals, houses, family land, or land they had purchased to the service of the temple. In most cases, however, an equivalent value or price was paid to the priest for the person or thing being dedicated. When the price had been paid, the person or thing was said to have been redeemed:

> "If you make a vow to the LORD your God, do not be slow to pay it, for the LORD your God will certainly demand it of you and you will be guilty of sin. But if you refrain from making a vow, you will not be guilty. Whatever your lips utter you must be sure to do, because you made your vow freely to the LORD your God with your own mouth"
>
> (Deut 23:21-23 KJV).

NEW TESTAMENT VOWS

There are five mentions of *vows* on three different topics in the New Testament. Jesus and Paul talks about the seriousness of *marriage vows* in the Book of Matthew and 1ˢᵗ Corinthians (Matthew 19:3-12; 1 Corinthians 7:1-16). The Nazarite Vow is mentioned twice in the Book of Acts (Acts 18:18, 21:15-26) and there is mention of a vow taken by forty men who bound themselves to a curse not to eat nor drink until they had killed Paul (Acts 23:12-24).

> "And Paul after this tarried there yet a good while, and then took his leave of the brethren, and sailed

thence into Syria, and with him Priscilla and Aquila;
having shorn his head in Cenchrea: for he had a
vow."

(Acts 18:18 KJV)

FIRST MENTION OF THE NAZARITE VOW

The Apostle Paul knew that he was under grace and no
longer under the Law of Moses. This was an exercise
of his Christian liberty. It was not an obligation. It is
the same as a Vow of Commitment today. It is *not* an
obligation for the believer. The Book of Peter clearly
states, 'But you are a chosen generation, a royal priest-
hood, a holy nation. His own special people that you
may proclaim the praises of Him who called you out of
darkness into His marvelous light. Who once was not
a people but are now the people of God who had not
obtained mercy, but now have obtained mercy (1 Peter
2:9-10, *emphasis mine*). Cenchrea is the eastern port of
Corinth. It is not specifically stated why Paul took the
Nazarite Vow, but it can always be concluded that it
was in preparation of the upcoming feast and a sign of
being grateful and dedicated to serving God:

> "1 And the LORD spake unto Moses, saying, 2 Speak
> unto the children of Israel, and say unto them, When
> either man or woman shall separate themselves to
> vow a vow of a Nazarite, to separate themselves unto
> the LORD: 3 He shall separate himself from wine and
> strong drink, and shall drink no vinegar of wine, or
> vinegar of strong drink, neither shall he drink any
> liquor of grapes, nor eat moist grapes, or dried. 4 All
> the days of his separation shall he eat nothing that

is made of the vine tree, from the kernels even to the husk. 5 All the days of the vow of his separation there shall no razor come upon his head: until the days be fulfilled, in the which he separateth himself unto the LORD, he shall be holy, and shall let the locks of the hair of his head grow. 6 All the days that he separateth himself unto the LORD he shall come at no dead body. 7 He shall not make himself unclean for his father, or for his mother, for his brother, or for his sister, when they die: because the consecration of his God is upon his head. 8 All the days of his separation he is holy unto the LORD."

(Num 6:1-8 KJV)

The shaving of the head prior to making the vow the and shaving of the head after the specific time correlates to a 30 day separation unto God in which the person making the vow had to be back at the temple prior to the completion of the thirty days to offer the hair that grew back as a sacrifice to God. The Vow could be any length of time the person specified. The average time was for thirty days of fasting and praying in the temple. The shaving of the head was an obvious sign of the Nazarite Vow and public declaration of consecrated service to God. One full week of the vow had to be spent in the temple in total dedication to the Lord. Those who were able to stay in the temple for the full thirty days were financially supported by wealthy people (as we shall discover during Paul's third missionary journey). There was a separate place in the temple for those who took the Nazarite Vow to worship called the Nazarites Court. There are at least three men mentioned in the Bible who undertook the Nazarite

Vow for life of whom a razor never touched their heads. They were Sampson, the Prophet Samuel, and John the Baptist. This first mention of the Nazarite Vow in the New Testament took place during Paul's second missionary journey. Paul's second missionary journey covered twenty-eight hundred miles. As Paul endeavored to visit the churches he had planted before attending one of the three feasts in Jerusalem, his thirty-day journey from Corinth covered about fifteen hundred miles before arriving in Jerusalem for the feast.

SECOND MENTION OF THE NAZARITE VOW

During Paul's third missionary journey we encounter the second mention of the Nazarite Vow (Acts 21:15-26).

"15 And after those days we took up our carriages, and went up to Jerusalem. 16 There went with us also certain of the disciples of Caesarea, and brought with them one Mnason of Cyprus, an old disciple, with whom we should lodge. 17 And when we were come to Jerusalem, the brethren received us gladly. 18 And the day following Paul went in with us unto James; and all the elders were present. 19 And when he had saluted them, he declared particularly what things God had wrought among the Gentiles by his ministry. 20 And when they heard it, they glorified the LORD, and said unto him, Thou seest, brother, how many thousands of Jews there are which believe; and they are all zealous of the law: 21 And they are informed of thee, that thou teachest all the Jews which are among the Gentiles to forsake

Moses, saying that they ought not to circumcise their children, neither to walk after the customs. 22 What is it therefore? the multitude must needs come together: for they will hear that thou art come. 23 Do therefore this that we say to thee: We have four men which have a vow on them; 24 Them take, and purify thyself with them, and be at charges with them, that they may shave their heads: and all may know that those things, whereof they were informed concerning thee, are nothing; but that thou thyself also walkest orderly, and keepest the law. 25 As touching the Gentiles which believe, we have written and concluded that they observe no such thing, save only that they keep themselves from things offered to idols, and from blood, and from strangled, and from fornication. 26 Then Paul took the men, and the next day purifying himself with them entered into the temple, to signify the accomplishment of the days of purification, until that an offering should be offered for every one of them."

(Acts 21:15-26 KJV)

By this time in Jerusalem, there were thousands of Christians who were mixing Christianity with Judaism. They were zealous of the Law. They were continuing in the rights of Judaism. They were continuing in the Law of Moses though they did believe that Jesus Christ was the Messiah. It appears the church elders had accommodated themselves to the Jewish community and so they said, 'they had been informed about you [Paul], that you are teaching all the Jews that are among the gentiles to forsake Moses; saying they ought not to circumcise their children, neither to walk after the customs. Now, what is it therefore? You see, when the multitude come together, they are going to have to find out about you because they're going to hear that you've come here. Now, this is what we'd like you to do. We have four men who have a vow on them. So take them and purify yourself with them and take care of their expenses that they may shave their heads and all may know things whereof they were informed about you are really nothing, but you yourself are a good Jewish boy living kosher. That they may know that you are walking orderly and keeping the law. We can clearly see that the church in Jerusalem was trying to keep from having an uproar during the feast. Rome had a great presence during the Jewish Feasts because of the possibility of an uprising of the people against Rome and Rome wanted to squash any such rebellion. The church in Jerusalem was diffinantly in a weakened state. Whenever the church seeks to adapt itself to the environment around it, the church always finds itself in a weakened state. One of the great curses of the church is its endeavor to adapt itself to the world that we might live in peace and harmony with the world. Jesus is such that there can be no mutual co-existence with sin. There can be no compromise with the world. The word of God says for believers to 'come out from them, be ye separate saith the Lord. Touch not the unclean thing and I will be a Father unto you and you shall be my sons and daughters (2 Cor 6:17-18, *emphasis mine*).

The LORD calls for a real separation, a real commitment. "We don't want any trouble Paul, now they've heard that you've been teaching that the Jews don't have to worry about the Law, just go ahead Paul and serve Jesus Christ, but hey, do us a favor, don't cause any trouble. All of these Jews are going to hear that you've come here and things are going to get a little sticky. Here are these four fellas and they come for the feast and they want to take a vow, so go with them and sponsor them."

Now, in taking the vow, you had to go a whole week, just in dedication to the Lord. It was a Nazarite Vow and you were suppose to take one week off and just spend the week in the temple, just worshipping God. Jewish customs and traditions teaches that those who took the Nazarite Vow had a hard time taking the week off to spend in the temple because they needed supplies and so they often had wealthy people who would sponsor them. Therefore, the church elders asked Paul to sponsor these four people. You have to admire Paul because he went along with the church elders and did it. Maybe he did it to follow his own exhortation in his Roman Epistle to live peaceably with all men (Roman 12:18, *emphasis mine*). If it would help them--fine. It shows the graciousness of Paul that he would go along with this suggestion knowing that he was free from these things. Paul knew the grace of God, something the church in Jerusalem had not discovered. They were still trying to please God by adherence to the Law, rather than obtaining to that righteousness that is by faith in Jesus Christ of which Paul wrote to the Romans that the Jews has a zeal for God, but not according to knowledge because they were ignorant of the righteousness that God has provided. And being ignorant of that righteousness they're going about trying to establish their own righteousness by the Law. The gentile Christians, expectedly were ignorant of the

Jewish laws. They obtained salvation by faith in Jesus Christ and thus they have experienced and entered into the blessings of the grace of God.

Paul paid the tab for these four guys and he shaved his head. The church council in Jerusalem had concluded that the Jews were not going to force on the Jews the Law's of Moses which their father's could not keep, but that they should keep from idols, from things strangled, and from fornication. Therefore, Paul took them in the next day and he purified himself and with them and he entered into the temple to signify the accomplishment of the days of purification until an offering should be offered for every one of them. Now, surely Paul would not have offered a 'sin offering' because he knew that that was already accomplished once and for all at the cross. However, there were other offerings that would have been legitimate for a Christian to offer. These were the 'burnt' offering, which was the offering of consecration. This offering was offered to God long before God gave the Law to Moses in the wilderness. The first mention of the *burnt* offering is in the Book of Genesis, when God told Abraham to sacrifice Isaac (Genesis 22:2). The 'meal' offerings (Lev 2:1-16), represents communion with God (also called the *meat* offering). Thus, we have in the New Testament the Lord's Supper, which represents communion with the Savior. Then there was the *drink* offering and the *heave* offering (offerings which we will not get into). I will note that in the world today, gang members pour *drink* offerings in honor of their dead.

The Kingdom Age, known as the Millennium Rein of Christ, speaks of offering sacrifices unto God:

"And it shall come to pass, that every one that is left of all the nations which came against Jerusalem shall even go up from year to year to worship the King, the Lord of hosts, and to keep the feast of tabernacles. 17 And it shall be, that whoso will not come up of all the families of the earth unto Jerusalem to worship the King, the Lord of hosts, even upon them shall be no rain. 18 And if the family of Egypt go not up, and come not, that have no rain; there shall be the plague, wherewith the Lord will smite the heathen that come not up to keep the feast of tabernacles. 19 This shall be the punishment of Egypt, and the punishment of all nations that come not up to keep the feast of tabernacles. 20 In that day shall there be upon the bells of the horses, HOLINESS UNTO THE Lord; and the pots in the Lord'S house shall be like the bowls before the altar. 21 Yea, every pot in Jerusalem and in Judah shall be holiness unto the Lord of hosts: and all they that sacrifice shall come and take of them, and seethe therein: and in that day there shall be no more the Canaanite in the house of the Lord of hosts."

(Zech 14:16-21 kjv)

The Kingdom Age speaks of *all* nations coming yearly to Jerusalem to keep the Feast of Tabernacle (one of the three feasts Paul endeavored to keep at Jerusalem) and it speaks of sacrifices that will be performed. They will no doubt probably be the *peace* offering, the *burnt* offerings, and the *meal* offering, but not the 'sin' offering, which was offered once and for all by Jesus on the cross. I know, I know, some of you are saying, 'I thought Jesus did away with all of the offering.' Well, as I understand it, the church will be removed in the

Rapture and God will once again turn his attention back to the Jews and sacrifices was what orthodox Jews were doing at Jesus' first coming. Hey, it's God' program and He can do whatever He wants. Remember, at Jesus' first coming, the Jews wanted Jesus to set up the kingdom and overthrow Rome. Well, at Jesus' second coming, He will overthrow a *revived* Roman Empire (Daniels feet of Iron mixed with Clay prophecy (Daniel 2:41-45), and set up the millennium Kingdom.

THIS IS THE POWER AND WISDOM OF GOD.

When Jesus came the first time, Rome was in charge. God, in essence, will pick up with the Jews where he left off when Jesus died on the cross for the sins of the world. At Jesus' second coming (Second Advent), a revived Roman Empire will be in place and led by the Anti-Christ, with the Jews back in their rebuilt temple--performing sacrifices. It's as if God halted time and picks it back up again with the Jews in completing the 70th Week of Daniel. Awesome.

THE MAKING OF A VOW OF COMMITMENT

A Vow of Commitment is similar, but not the same as the Nazarite Vow. It is not the same because we are not under the Law. We are under grace. We do not do animal sacrifices in the Body of Christ. A Vow of Commitment is primarily for *procrastinators*. It is a way of moving Christians under *grace* out of their comfort zone and into action. A Vow of Commitment must be challenging to be meaningful. Instead of animal sacrifices, the equivalent sacrifice would be not indulging yourself with the pleasures of this world (beauty shop, haircut, new cloths, shoes, etc...) during the vow. As Deuteronomy states, something of value had to be pledged and it was redeemed upon completion of the vow. Many of us can easily go six months to a year without new clothes and shoes (maybe just men). During this period of consecration to God, buy only the necessary necessities like food (except the fruit of the vine), medicine, and toiletries. There is to be no drinking of alcohol of any type...Period! Not even medicine with alcohol in it. There is to be no eating anything of the vine (including raisins). This is because the Lord Himself is to be your joy.

No alcohol. Alcohol is mentioned as one of the possible reason Nadab and Abihu, sons of Aaron the priest, was killed when they offered strange fire unto the LORD (Lev 10:1-7). The Glory of the Lord appeared to all the people and fire came out from before the Lord and consumed the altar, the burnt offering, and all of its fat. Maybe, just maybe, in all the excitement, they wanted to steal some attention for themselves. Maybe they genuinely wanted to bless God. Maybe Satan put them up to it, whatever the reason... they did that which they were commanded not to. Since God mentions alcohol in this passage of scripture, maybe they were under the influence of alcohol:

> "And the LORD spake unto Aaron, saying, 9 Do not drink wine nor strong drink, thou, nor thy sons with thee, when ye go into the tabernacle of the congregation, lest ye die: it shall be a statute for ever throughout your generations: 10 And that ye may put differ-

ence between holy and unholy, and between unclean and clean; 11 And that ye may teach the children of Israel all the statutes which the LORD hath spoken unto them by the hand of Moses"

(Lev 10:8-11 KJV).

Alcohol is a vehicle for Satan to manipulate your mind. God instructed the Priests not to drink while ministering at the tabernacle before God. Pastors of churches minister 24/7. In my opinion, drinking is not an option for pastors of churches (1 Tim 3:1-7). While under the influence of alcohol, he or she may think they are hearing from God when they are actually hearing from Satan. Alcohol is an open door to satanic attack, spiritual bondage, and physical addiction. For this reason, God commanded the priests not to drink while in service to the Lord. I personally do not understand how a person can drink wine and study the Bible at the same time (this is the *lukewarm* direction the church is headed). The gospel is not to be compromised. Satan does his best to compromise the gospel. For this reason, James warns Bible teachers that they will receive the greater condemnation. I have great fear in writing this book because I do not want to put anyone under bondage. The Vow of Commitment is purely voluntarily and mainly for procrastinators to *jump start* them in ministry.

No cutting of the hair. The reason God did not allow those who took the Nazarite Vow to cut their hair was so it would be obvious that they had separated themselves to the Lord. Sampson is the most remembered Nazarite in the Bible. The Nazarite Vow was upon him from his birth. He admitted his strength was in his hair. Well… problem is—his strength was *not* in his hair, but in his covenant relationship with God. His hair was a sign of the covenant. When his hair was cut, the covenant was broken. Sampson stated himself to Delilah that if his hair was cut, he would be like any other man. In the Old Testament, circumcism was a sign of the covenant between Abraham and God. In marriage, the ring is the sign of a covenant between a husband and his wife. The New Testament means 'New Covenant'. For those of you who make a Vow of Commitment, simply wash, dry, brush and pin up your hair while you are partaking of the vow.

Touch no dead thing. This is due to your consecration (set apart) to the Lord. Aaron was not to touch his dead sons, nor was he even to mourn for them because what they did was evil in the sight of God. The people were gathered together to celebrate the appearance of fire from the Lord that consumed the burnt offering. What a deterrence Satan causes by trying to steal God's glory. The camp witnessed God kill two priests! Moses had Aaron's cousins carry out his two dead sons from the tabernacle. The camp was not to mourn, but celebrate the appearance of God's glory. Because of his consecration, Aaron could not even touch his own sons. I can clearly see Satan trying to steal God's glory through Nadab and Abihu. It is nothing new for Satan, as the god of this world, to try and take God's glory for himself. As Christians, we must make sure we give God *His* glory.

BREAKING THE VOW

"This is the law of the Nazirite who vows his offering to the LORD in accordance with his separation, in addition to whatever else he can afford. He must fulfill the vow he has made, according to the law of the Nazirite"

(Num 6:21 KJV).

There were remedies in the Book of Leviticus, Chapter 5, verses 4-6, if you *broke* your vow *knowingly* or *unknowingly*. It was called the 'Trespass' offering and the 'Sin' Offering. The Trespass offering included a confession of the sin. People sin knowingly and unknowingly. A *trespass* offering was for those who knowingly sinned. They might have been in an adulterous relationship and completely enjoying it. It is when they wanted to be *restored* to God that they went before the priest for the priest to offer a *trespass* offering for their sin. A Sin offering was for being born a sinner, and for things we may have done outside the norm or unknowingly. As much as we may try not to sin, we can still sin either physically, mentally or spiritually. In 1 John 1:9, we read:

"If we confess our sins, He is faithful and just to forgive us our sins and cleanse us from all unrighteousness."

(1 John 1:9 KJV)

There were also certain conditions a vow can be *voided* which is found in the Book of Numbers, Chapter 30, verses 1-16. If for some personal reason (other than voidable reasons found in Numbers 30:1-16) you find you cannot keep your vow, it will surely require some type of remedy to God. If a person wanted to redeem something of value they pledged to the Lord in the Old Testament, that person had to pay a fifth part the value of their pledge (20%):

> "If the owner wishes to redeem the animal, he must add a fifth to its value."
>
> (Lev 27:13 KJV)

Since we do not conduct animal sacrifices and we do not need a priest to confess our sins, the only remedy *"I"* can think of is a *monetary* consideration.

Considering how much you would have spent on clothes, food, hair, nails, etc…, during your thirty day, six months or one year vow, multiply that amount by five and give it to your church as an offering to God (this is not a tithe). Within six months to a year, a person can easily spend $1000.00 dollars on personal luxuries. Multiply that amount times five (20 %) and you will find it to be less painful to keep your vow.

TAKING THE VOW

> "When thou vowest a vow unto God, defer not to pay it; for he hath no pleasure in fools: pay that which thou hast vowed. 5 Better is it that thou shouldest not vow, than that thou shouldest vow and not pay.6 Suffer not thy mouth to cause thy flesh to sin; neither say thou before the angel, that it was an error: wherefore should God be angry at thy voice, and destroy the work of thine hands? 7 For in the multitude of dreams and many words there are also divers vanities: but fear thou God"
>
> (Eccl 5:4-7 KJV).

I want to tell you that anything you commit to the Lord has blessings that *far* outweigh the temporary sacrifices. Material things come and go; it is what we do for God that lasts. Personally, I long to hear Jesus say, 'Well done My good and faithful servant.'

> "I delight greatly in the LORD; my soul rejoices in my God. He has clothed me with garments of salvation and arrayed me in a robe of righteousness, as a bridegroom adorns his head like a priest, and as a bride adorns herself with her jewels"
>
> (Isaiah 61:10 KJV).

THE VOW OF COMMITMENT:

Pray:

Father God, Jehovah, on this day _____,of this month _____, of this year _____, and ending on this day _____, of this month _____, of this year _____, I _____, do 'freely' and 'intentionally' take upon myself a Vow of Commitment by volunteering for special duty to the Holy Trinity (Father, Son, Holy Spirit). It is my heart's desire to bring glory to your name Father and bear much fruit for the Kingdom of God. It is my heart's desire Lord Jesus to know You more intimately and fulfill my part of the *Great Commission* to reach the lost for Your Glory. It is also my heart's desire, Holy Spirit, to be a vessel of honor to you and to use the gifts You have given me to exalt the name of Jesus above every name of human origin, power, principality, dominion, and kingdom. I will not purchase anything of material nature to glorify my flesh during my vow. I will buy only necessary toiletry items, medicine and food. Please Father, accept my offer of special service to you and *grow* me, *stretch* me, and *mold* me into the Child of God You created me to be.

Chapter 9

ENDING THE VOW

"And this is the law of the Nazarite, when the days of
his separation are fulfilled: he shall be brought unto
the door of the tabernacle of the congregation"
(Numbers 6:13-21 KJV).

There is no public ceremony. We are not under the
Law. We do not do conduct the *Burnt* offering, the *Sin*
offering, nor the *Trespass* offering. We do not cut our
hair and burn it. You can go boldly before the Throne
of Grace on your own behalf. In the final analysis, you
will have a *Satisfaction* within your spirit that may
never have been obtained without the Vow. You will
have entered *Spiritual Warfare* for the souls of others.
You will have obtained *Discipline*. You will have grown
in *Spiritual Maturity*. You will be able to see life better
through the *Eyes* of God. You will have a better understanding of the *Heart* of God. You will be able to better
hear the *Voice* of God. You will have partaken in the
Great Commission. You will have stepped out on *Faith,
and* you will have increased your faith *and* prayerfully,
you will do it again next year.

Warning

While you were on your vow, the enemy attacked you, but you were on high alert and your spiritual antenna was up. You were watching and waiting for Satan's attack. He tried to consume your time in order to make it difficult to accomplish your mission. If we look at the life of a pastor on a Sunday morning, while the pastor is preaching, they are focused on the message but the enemy still tries to distract them. What Satan does is use the congregation in an attempt to interrupt or distract as much as possible from his/her message. Have you noticed how, right before it is time to give an offering and/or the Bible message, and/or Alter call, how people have to use the bathroom? This is a major distraction for a pastor, especially during the offering of salvation following their message. After the preacher has preached is when he or she is most vulnerable to attacks. The same goes for you, now that your vow is completed, you yourself will be in this vulnerable position. Satan will come at you with a different strategies to prevent you from making any future vows.

Journal

I have made available a journal to compliment this book. It is imperative to daily annotate your spiritual challenges. List your greatest challenges first and how God provided for you. It will be an awesome reminder of how God opened closed doors, did the unusual, communed with you, and strengthened your flesh and your spirit. You can reflect on how you have grown in the study of God's word, how your faith had increased and your personal devotion time, to include how you now see the lost and your role in God's plan of salvation.

Endnotes

1. Dr. J. Vernon McGee, *Thru the Bible Radio Broadcast*, www.ttb.org, Christian radio station, KELP, AM 1590, EL Paso, TX.

2. Tim LaHaye, Jerry B. Jenkins, *Left Behind*, (Carol Stream, IL: Tyndale House, 2005).

3. Jim Carrey, *Bruce Almighty*, (Universal Studios, 2002).

4. All text is available under the terms of the GNU Free Documentation License. Wikipedia® is a registered trademark of the Wikimedia Foundation, Inc., a US-registered 501(c)(3) tax-deductible nonprofit charity.

5. NLT, *New Living Translation*, (Tyndale House Publishers, 2005).

6. Bishop T. D. Jakes, *Woman Thou Art Loosed*, (New York, NY: Berkley Trade Pbk. Ed edition, 2004).

7. Christian Radio, To Every Man An Answer, (EL Paso, TX: KELP, AM 1590, 2007).

Resources

(www.thenazaritevow.com)

(www.zealousforsouls.org)

(www.faithbasedcounseling.com)

(www.backtojerusalem.com)
Book: The Heavenly Man

(www.persecution.com)
Voice of the Martyrs

(www.donpiperministry.com)
Book: 90 Minutes in Heaven

(www.liberty.edu)
Liberty Theological University

Biography

Reverend Zachary F. Hooey attends Northeast Bible Fellowship Church where he is the church administrator. He attended Sun City Christian Fellowship Baptist Church where he was over the Men's Ministry program for over four years. He was one of a few ministers on the roster to include his wife, Reverend Irene D. Hooey. He is a retired Army Soldier with 25 years of Active Duty Service. He joined the Army at the age of 17 while attending James Madison Sr. High School on January 20, 1979 (the same high school quarterback Vince Young graduated from). He retired on August 1, 2004, out of FT Bliss, TX. His last duty assignment was a *Battle Staff Instructor* at the Sergeants Major Academy. He is currently working at FT Bliss, TX, and as a Real Estate Salesman and a Mortgage Loan Officer. He was the host of Get Right *NOW*, a live radio broadcast on EL Paso's Christian radio station, KELP, AM 1590, for over two years. He is currently pursuing a Masters Degree in Pastoral Counseling from Liberty University (Distance Education), Lynchburg, VA. In addition to pursuing a Masters Degree, he has completed the following certification courses from the Faith Based Counselor Training Institute: The Basic Certification Course and the Advanced Certification Course consisting of Anger Management Specialist, Certified Chemical Dependency Counselor, Crisis Chaplaincy,

Youth Violence Intervention Specialist, and Complex Family Issues. He recently joined Hospice of El Paso, TX, in July of 2007. It has been and always will be his desire to give God more to work with and it is his hope and prayer that this book will inspire you to strive to give God more to work with in ministry.

January

Day

1 _____

2 _____

3 _____

4 _____

5 _____

6 _____

7 _____

8 _____

9 _____

10 _____

11 _____

12 _____

13 _____
_____
_____
_____
_____

14 _____
_____
_____
_____

15 _____
_____
_____
_____

16 _____
_____
_____
_____

17 _____
_____
_____
_____

18 _____
_____
_____
_____

19 _____
_____
_____

20 _____

21 _____

22 _____

23 _____

24 _____

25 _____

26 _____
_____
_____
_____
_____
27 _____
_____
_____
_____
_____
28 _____
_____
_____
_____
_____
29 _____
_____
_____
_____
_____
30 _____
_____
_____
_____
_____
31 _____
_____
_____
_____
_____

February

Day

1

2

3

4

5

6

7

8

9

10

11

12

13 _____
_____
_____
_____
_____

14 _____
_____
_____
_____

15 _____
_____
_____
_____

16 _____
_____
_____
_____

17 _____
_____
_____

18 _____
_____
_____

19 _____
_____

20

21

22

23

24

25

26 _____
_____
_____
_____
_____
27 _____
_____
_____
_____
28 _____
_____
_____
_____
29 _____
_____
_____
_____
_____

March

Day

1 _____
_____
_____
_____
_____

2 _____
_____
_____
_____
_____

3 _____
_____
_____
_____
_____

4 _____
_____
_____
_____
_____

5 _____
_____
_____
_____
_____

6 _____
_____

7

8

9

10

11

12

13 _____
_____
_____
_____
_____

14 _____
_____
_____
_____
_____

15 _____
_____
_____
_____
_____

16 _____
_____
_____
_____
_____

17 _____
_____
_____
_____
_____

18 _____
_____
_____
_____
_____

19 _____
_____

20 _____

21 _____

22 _____

23 _____

24 _____

25 _____

26 _____

27 _____

28 _____

29 _____

30 _____

31 _____

April

Day

1

2

3

4

5

6

7 _____

8 _____

9 _____

10 _____

11 _____

12 _____

13 _____
_____
_____
_____
_____

14 _____
_____
_____
_____

15 _____
_____
_____
_____

16 _____
_____
_____
_____

17 _____
_____
_____
_____

18 _____
_____
_____
_____

19 _____
_____

20

21

22

23

24

25

26 _____
_____
_____
_____
_____

27 _____
_____
_____
_____
_____

28 _____
_____
_____
_____
_____

29 _____
_____
_____
_____
_____

30 _____
_____
_____
_____
_____

May

Day

1 _____
 _____
 _____
 _____

2 _____
 _____
 _____
 _____

3 _____
 _____
 _____
 _____

4 _____
 _____
 _____
 _____

5 _____
 _____
 _____
 _____

6 _____
 _____

7

8

9

10

11

12

13 _____
_____
_____
_____
_____

14 _____
_____
_____
_____

15 _____
_____
_____

16 _____
_____
_____

17 _____
_____
_____

18 _____
_____
_____

19 _____
_____

20 _____

21 _____

22 _____

23 _____

24 _____

25 _____

26 _____

27 _____

28 _____

29 _____

30 _____

31 _____

June

Day

1

2

3

4

5

6

7 _____

8 _____

9 _____

10 _____

11 _____

12 _____

13 _____
   _____
   _____
   _____
   _____

14 _____
   _____
   _____
   _____
   _____

15 _____
   _____
   _____
   _____
   _____

16 _____
   _____
   _____
   _____
   _____

17 _____
   _____
   _____
   _____
   _____

18 _____
   _____
   _____
   _____
   _____

19 _____
   _____

_____
_____
_____
20 _____
_____
_____
_____
_____
21 _____
_____
_____
_____
22 _____
_____
_____
_____
23 _____
_____
_____
_____
24 _____
_____
_____
_____
25 _____
_____
_____
_____
_____

26 _____
_____
_____
_____

27 _____
_____
_____
_____

28 _____
_____
_____
_____

29 _____
_____
_____
_____

30 _____
_____
_____
_____

July

Day

1 _____

2 _____

3 _____

4 _____

5 _____

6 _____

7

8

9

10

11

12

13 _____

_____

_____

_____

14 _____

_____

_____

_____

15 _____

_____

_____

_____

16 _____

_____

_____

_____

17 _____

_____

_____

_____

18 _____

_____

_____

_____

19 _____

_____

20

21

22

23

24

25

26 _____
_____
_____
_____
_____
27 _____
_____
_____
_____
_____
28 _____
_____
_____
_____
_____
29 _____
_____
_____
_____
_____
30 _____
_____
_____
_____
_____
31 _____
_____
_____
_____
_____

Day

1

2

3

4

5

6

7

8

9

10

11

12

13 _____
_____
_____
_____
_____
14 _____
_____
_____
_____
_____
15 _____
_____
_____
_____
_____
16 _____
_____
_____
_____
_____
17 _____
_____
_____
_____
_____
18 _____
_____
_____
_____
_____
19 _____
_____

20

21

22

23

24

25

26 _____

27 _____

28 _____

29 _____

30 _____

31 _____

September

Day

1

2

3

4

5

6

7

8

9

10

11

12

13 _____
_____
_____
_____
_____

14 _____
_____
_____
_____
_____

15 _____
_____
_____
_____
_____

16 _____
_____
_____
_____
_____

17 _____
_____
_____
_____
_____

18 _____
_____
_____
_____
_____

19 _____
_____

20 _____

21 _____

22 _____

23 _____

24 _____

25 _____

26 _____
_____
_____
_____

27 _____
_____
_____
_____

28 _____
_____
_____
_____

29 _____
_____
_____
_____

30 _____
_____
_____
_____

Ocotober

Day

1 _____

2 _____

3 _____

4 _____

5 _____

6 _____

7

8

9

10

11

12

13 _____
  _____
  _____
  _____
  _____
14 _____
  _____
  _____
  _____
  _____
15 _____
  _____
  _____
  _____
  _____
16 _____
  _____
  _____
  _____
  _____
17 _____
  _____
  _____
  _____
  _____
18 _____
  _____
  _____
  _____
  _____
19 _____
  _____

20 _____

21 _____

22 _____

23 _____

24 _____

25 _____

26 _____

_____

_____

_____

_____

27 _____

_____

_____

_____

28 _____

_____

_____

_____

29 _____

_____

_____

_____

30 _____

_____

_____

_____

31 _____

_____

_____

_____

Day

1 _____
_____
_____
_____
_____

2 _____
_____
_____
_____
_____

3 _____
_____
_____
_____
_____

4 _____
_____
_____
_____
_____

5 _____
_____
_____
_____
_____

6 _____
_____
_____

7

8

9

10

11

12

13 _____
_____
_____
_____
_____

14 _____
_____
_____
_____
_____

15 _____
_____
_____
_____

16 _____
_____
_____
_____

17 _____
_____
_____
_____

18 _____
_____
_____
_____

19 _____
_____

20

21

22

23

24

25

26 _____

_____

_____

_____

_____

27 _____

_____

_____

_____

28 _____

_____

_____

_____

29 _____

_____

_____

_____

30 _____

_____

_____

_____

_____

December

Day

1 _____
_____
_____
_____
_____

2 _____
_____
_____
_____

3 _____
_____
_____
_____

4 _____
_____
_____
_____

5 _____
_____
_____
_____

6 _____
_____
_____
_____

7 _____

8 _____

9 _____

10 _____

11 _____

12 _____

13 _____
_____
_____
_____
_____

14 _____
_____
_____
_____
_____

15 _____
_____
_____
_____
_____

16 _____
_____
_____
_____
_____

17 _____
_____
_____
_____
_____

18 _____
_____
_____
_____
_____

19 _____
_____

20 _____

21 _____

22 _____

23 _____

24 _____

25 _____

26 _____

_____

_____

_____

_____

27 _____

_____

_____

_____

28 _____

_____

_____

_____

29 _____

_____

_____

_____

30 _____

_____

_____

_____

31 _____

_____

_____

_____